Chasing Thin Shadows:

A Beginner's Guide to Paranormal Investigating

Kimberly,
Thank you for the
opportunity to be your friend!
Michael

MICHAEL H. WHITE

DEDICATION

I dedicate this revised handbook to Katie Jones, Matthew Quesada, Lilla Bodo, and "Michael's Minions." Your friendship and support have always, and will always, mean everything to me.

CONTENTS

ACKNOWLEDGMENTS

This handbook would not be possible without the knowledge and friendship of an entire community of paranormal investigators. Shared information from each paranormal investigation makes us more informed, more aware, and more efficient, while we stalk the unseen in the dark!

1 INTRODUCTION

Every paranormal investigator started out with a first investigation. He or she may have had no equipment or had purchased some equipment with the hopes of experiencing and capturing an apparition, disembodied voice, or any other paranormal interaction. Some have been lucky enough to get real "evidence" of paranormal activity on their first investigation while others have not. In any case, the first-time paranormal investigator is usually armed with plenty of ambition. Taking that ambition, combining it with organizational skills, knowledge of equipment, understanding of investigative procedures, and effective sharing of collected evidence, will give you and your team credibility. Credibility is everything in the paranormal community!

You are entering into a field where there are innumerable amounts of beliefs, opinions, and speculations, and no doubt you already have some of your own. The paranormal community is full of experienced and inexperienced people with their own ideas, methods, and understanding of paranormal phenomena, and there really is no one right way of doing anything. Some people hold very rigid ideas on what paranormal activity represents - some that may differ completely from your own; hearing them out is a great way to remain balanced and objective.

Paranormal investigation is a field of study for some, and a hobby for others, but the common denominator is that it can be an interesting and exciting activity no matter what the approach is! As with any exciting activity, there are some dangers involved that you must be prepared for; this handbook will help you identify some of them.

Paranormal investigating is multifaceted. The word "paranormal" addresses any subject outside of our scientifically defined reality. Interests that fall within the paranormal realm can include, and are not limited to: extrasensory perception (ESP), unidentified flying objects (UFOs), astral projection, telekinesis, cryptozoology, and so much more. This handbook specifically targets paranormal investigations of residences and other buildings and grounds where the reported activity suggests that a disembodied entity may be involved. Using popular terminology, this handbook is about ghost hunting.

The public thinks that every paranormal investigator is a ghost hunter. The term "ghost hunter" in my opinion, is not as accurate as the term "paranormal investigator." To me, "ghost hunting" suggests that you are tracking down or lying in wait until a ghost comes along so you can seize it. Few paranormal investigators have a prize trophy of a ghost mounted on their wall. More often than not, your investigation will find a logical explanation for some, if not all, of the reported activity. There are times when your findings defy logic or scientific explanation. When you find that unexplainable piece of data that pegs your *weird-shit-o'meter*, it makes all of the time you spent investigating more interesting.

The intent of this handbook is to assist the curious novice interested in conducting paranormal investigations with enough information to get started in the practice successfully. Within these pages you will be challenged to discover your own reasons for becoming a paranormal investigator, and you will be presented with a brief overview of investigative equipment. You will also find some procedural guidance on preparing for and conducting investigations, scrutinizing data, and presenting evidence. Essentially, this loosely written procedure manual is flexible enough to be adapted to many types of investigations. I have also included a few useful forms to get you started with your first couple of investigations.

The investigative methods and philosophies that this handbook presents are not intended to belittle any other investigative methods or philosophies; they merely are presented to provide the novice investigator with a place to start. Every team has their own procedures of conducting their investigation, whether they are formal or informal. If you intend to join an established team and you have read this book, then you have already become a valuable asset to that team. If you are flying solo or forming your own investigation team, you are more than welcome to adopt these procedures or adapt them to your own philosophies and beliefs. Eventually, you will discover what works for you and your team, and you will devise your own methods.

This handbook was written for you to be successful on your first and subsequent investigations. However, this book does not define what success is; only you can do that. Success for some might be to walk into a location and successfully debunk every report of activity. Success for others might be that they walked away from an investigation with an autographed photo of Grover Cleveland signed that very evening! It is up to you how you define your success.

I would like to point out that you will see the words, "data," and "evidence" quite a few times within these pages. There is a difference! One word that you will not see is, "proof." For the most part, paranormal investigators present evidence and draw some possible conclusions using very loose interpretations of the scientific method.

Please note that I have written this book for the layperson. In most cases I have tried to keep everything as simple as possible so it is useful to a larger audience. I have also refrained from incorporating any spiritual or religious philosophies in this handbook. My intention is purely to guide you through the process of investigating the paranormal without any comment to its spiritual implications. Though I may throw a technical or psychological term into the mix of pages here, it is not my intention to dazzle you with brilliance or baffle you with bullshit. My intention is simply to give you useful information that will hopefully inspire you and give you realistic expectations. I have attempted to remove redundancies in all discussion points except for those points that I believe should be restated (which is a personal accomplishment for me as an honors graduate from the Academy of Redundancy Academy where I was Summa Cum Laude). You will find that this book is to the point with little attempt to decorate the page with fancy words, and I do not intend to insult your intelligence by clearly stating the obvious. Now turn the page to continue reading this book.

2 WHY DO YOU WANT TO BE A PARANORMAL INVESTIGATOR?

There is no right or wrong reason to get into investigating the paranormal. You undoubtedly have your own reasons already, or you would not have picked up this handbook. A simple curiosity for the unexplained phenomenon that you have witnessed, heard about, or have seen on television might be enough to motivate you into this field. It is important to completely understand and articulate your own motivations for getting into paranormal investigating. You must understand your own motivations because it is that understanding that will guide you into setting your own personal and/or team goals.

Though you may have seen "experts" on the numerous television shows using sophisticated equipment and explaining the unexplainable, the reality is that anyone can conduct a paranormal investigation. With nothing more than a limited understanding, usually gained by watching a season of popular ghost-hunting television shows, a person, or team can get what they call "evidence." However, is it really evidence? What is it evidence of? Is it evidence of paranormal activity? Does it prove the existence of an afterlife? What was the goal of the investigation? Many of these questions can be answered if the goal of the investigation is established well before the investigation takes place. The goal of the investigation should be derived from your personal and the team's motivation for conducting the investigation. Having a goal for each investigation brings objective meaning to the entire event.

Having a realistic understanding of yourself and a clear understanding of the goal or purpose of the investigation is vitally important. This understanding will bring meaning to the data that you collect during your investigation. The meaningful data that we as investigators collect is then called "evidence."

Each piece of evidence that is obtained and shared throughout the community is significant, but might not seem like it at the time. You are entering into a field that is like a giant jigsaw puzzle with a billion pieces. The entire puzzle is invisible, and it seems that it has no corners. This puzzle is built from the inside outward, and your approach to attempting to be a paranormal puzzle-solver must start from inside you. So, stop and think; "Why do I want to be a paranormal investigator?"

The realities of paranormal investigating:

Unlike the hour-long TV shows, investigating the paranormal is very time consuming! Each investigation can take several hours, if not days to prepare for, hours to conduct, and then even more time painstakingly reviewing all of the data. Refer to the example below:

A 5-hour investigation with 4 DVR cameras, 4 audio recorders, 1 handheld video camera, and assorted digital cameras will total at least:

5 hours – actual investigation
20 hours – review of 4 DVR cameras
20 hours – review of audio recorders
5 hours - review of video camera
2 hours – estimated review of digital photos

Total - 52 hours of your life spent just for conducting the investigation and evidence review. When you add the time of setting up the investigation with the location owner, travel time to and from the location, and how much time the reveal takes to prepare and present, you might be looking at several days of work. This field can be very time-consuming, and in 99% of cases, costly too! This is time and money that you will not get back. Understand that 99.99% of paranormal teams do not charge for their services.

Quite often, even with all of the time and effort you have put into it, an investigation might not yield any evidence at all! In all honesty, sometimes it can be very discouraging after you have invested so much of your time and effort, but you must keep in mind that the lack of evidence is not necessarily evidence of a lack of activity. It simply means that you did not document anything during your investigation. Every legitimate investigative team can honestly say that this happens, but hopefully not too often. Keep in mind that even in a location that has reports of a lot of paranormal activity spanning 50 years, it is doubtful that reported activity is happening 24 hours a day, 7 days a week. The five or more hours that you spend investigating that location would represent a very small fraction of time of the reported activity, so your odds of observing and documenting that activity are very slim.

At times, you might become frustrated by obtaining evidence that seems nonsensical. Sometimes, the evidence that you obtain does not seem to have anything to do with why you were called out to investigate originally. You might get an EVP of a little girl's voice in an area that used to be a prison, or a recording that sounds like boots walking on a wooden floor while investigating a field or cemetery. When these out-of-place events are recorded, you are better off presenting it as an unexplained event, especially if the historical research of the property does not support it. These anomalous pieces of data are often vague, and can be damaging to your or your team's credibility if you try too hard to give it meaning. Presenting your interpretation of a recorded event must be done with objectivity and be realistic. If you cannot explain a piece of evidence, don't try; a digital recording of sleigh bells in a location where no sleigh bells exist does not prove the existence of Santa Claus, nor does this recording prove the existence of Grandma's afterlife following her mishap with the reindeer! Keep it real; you have a recording that sounds like sleigh bells, and nothing more.

Investigations can be mentally and physically demanding on even the most seasoned investigators. Driving for hours to get to the location, setting up the equipment, conducting the investigation in the dark in unfamiliar territory, breaking down and correctly stowing all of the equipment, and then safely getting home can take a real toll on a person. It can be tough to investigate when everyone is already tired and cranky, not feeling well, it is too cold or too hot, or someone is just having a bad day. It happens to every team out there, and real-world events, like working hours, the weather, or the daily events in a person's life can really interfere with what could have been a good investigation. It can happen, it does happen, and it does affect the outcome of the investigation tremendously. The best thing to do with an investigation that did not go as planned is to identify all of the contributing factors and learn how to avoid or reduce them in future investigations. Sometimes a bad investigation is a good thing, because you can learn what not to do, what to avoid, or how to plan better the next time.

None of the above information is presented to discourage you from getting into paranormal investigating. You need to know the realities of the practice, not just how much fun and exciting it can be. There are many people that join or form paranormal teams without realizing how much time and effort it takes, and many of those people do not remain within the community for long. Most of them had no idea what was really expected of them; chances are that they did not have this book or any similar media to prepare them. Other people that have dropped out of the community simply did not have a clear understanding of their own motivations for entering in the first place. This is why it is so important to understand your own motivations. Better to have that understanding before you invest the time that it takes to do it adequately.

Do you have what it takes to be a paranormal investigator?

When getting into this field, the first step is to conduct an honest and accurate assessment of your personal qualifications. What are you personally bringing to the investigation? Or, what are you bringing to a paranormal team (whether this is a team you personally establish or an existing team of seasoned investigators)? Are you an honest person willing to bring forth evidence even if that evidence contradicts your own personal beliefs or preconceived notions? What traits do you possess that are valuable? The following is hardly an all-encompassing list, but here are some great traits to have for this field:

Honesty and integrity: In my opinion, these are the most important traits to possess in this, and every other field. You must be truthful with your team, clients, the public, and above all else, yourself. You will find yourself in many situations where your mind will play tricks on you, and lead you to believe that things are occurring when they are not. You must be honest with yourself and not embellish what you see or hear. You will also be trusted with expensive equipment, entrusted with someone's home or business, and you must value that trust and use the utmost caution to protect those investments.

Open-mindedness: Do not go to an investigation with preconceived ideas of what you are going to experience – you must be completely open to whatever may or may NOT happen. Observed occurrences might conflict with your current beliefs; be prepared for that. In addition, you might be working with team members or clients who - because of their beliefs - might perceive the situation from a different perspective than you do. You must remain respectful of those beliefs even if they do not correspond with your own.

The ability to remain positive: This trait alone can salvage an investigation when it seems that nothing is going as planned. Negativity is contagious and can ruin an investigation. Maintaining a positive attitude promotes problem solving, esteem, and keeps everyone motivated.

Critical thinking: If something looks like a duck and quacks like a duck, instead of just accepting that it is a duck, try to figure out if it is truly a duck and how it might have come to be in the space (this is especially important in normally duck-less environments).

Having some investigative skills certainly makes you a more valuable member of any team. There are skills, many more than this short list of examples that are instrumental on a successful investigation. These are some of the most obvious skills.

Equipment knowledge: Knowing the capabilities and proper use of the equipment will significantly improve the quality of the data received from them.

Interpersonal skills: Knowing how to deal with people will ensure that the dealings with the client, other team members, the general public, and possible unseen entities remains positive.

Sensitivity: This ability has wide-ranging implications. Being sensitive can merely mean that you are able to gauge the emotional state of others, or, it can mean that you feel the presence of others that cannot be seen. In either case, it is a valuable ability.

Observational skills: Our five senses, and a possible sixth, determine the perceived reality that we experience in the present, and form our perspective of the immediate and subsequent situations. Having good eyesight (especially good night vision), good hearing, adequate sense of smell and touch are vital to the investigation process. Most of the time, one or more of your senses will alert you to a general or specific area to investigate, record, take a specific reading, or photograph. Trust your senses.

Problem-solving skills: Being able to assess a problem or situation, identifying all of the contributing factors, and presenting possible solutions lead to an explanation. Sometimes the simplest explanations are the most accurate.

There is no standard skill set that is a best fit for every investigation, because every investigation is different. The best-case scenario for any investigation is to have an investigative team, where each team member brings a unique skill set to the party that works efficiently to achieve the investigative goal(s). With an accurate assessment of your own motivations and capabilities, you increase your chances of being a successful ghost hunter or paranormal investigator, depending on what you want to call yourself.

A very important thing to remember: paranormal investigating is a lot like fishing. You might have the best fishing equipment in the world, calm waters, perfect weather conditions, but not catch any fish (and just because you did not catch any fish, it does not mean that there are no fish to catch). In addition, like fishing, if you approach each fishing trip cheerfully, plan carefully, and hope realistically for a good catch, you have at least guaranteed yourself a good time.

3 PARANORMAL INVESTIGATION EQUIPMENT

Although I have a lifetime of finding myself in areas that had paranormal activity worldwide, I did not have any equipment at the time. Sadly, all of my experiences can be summed up as mere ghost stories because I did not have any documentation to back up what I experienced. I also could not distinguish whether the events that took place on my travels were truly paranormal events, figments of my overactive imagination, or some natural occurrences in the immediate environment.

My paranormal excursions were simply incidental to the locations that I found myself while serving in the U.S. Navy. Liberty call in each port would allow me to search for, and usually find, the creepiest place that seemed to call to me. Therefore, during that period of my life, I was not really a paranormal investigator as much as just another paranormal thrill-seeker. Oddly enough, I learned that many of the feelings and experiences that I had during those years were very similar to those that I have had as a serious paranormal investigator, so even though they went undocumented, they were valid experiences. I also learned that strange events and what could be classified as paranormal activity can happen anywhere, not just in old creepy houses, cemeteries, forts, and museums. I've experienced strange occurrences at Caribbean beaches, a rum factory, jungles in Guam, alleys in France and Hong Kong, a fish and chips joint in Scotland, a movie theater in Japan, a hospital in the Middle East, a food storage room onboard one of the submarines I was attached to, and in a home in Tarawa. But because I was not carrying any investigative equipment that would capture, quantify, and document these events, they are simply eerie memories of strange days gone by.

When I first started seriously investigating, I did not have a budget that would allow for purchasing a lot of investigative equipment. Because I grew up in a family that did not have much money I learned to make due with what I had, and I am glad as it made me more resourceful. I made what I needed, or purchased whatever I was able to afford, and made it work. I constructed my own paranormal equipment kit at a much lower cost than many prepackaged starter kits. I had a digital camera that also had video capability, a digital voice recorder, a laser instant-read thermometer (that I normally used for cooking), and a compass (I used the deflection of the needle to determine the presence of electromagnetic fields). Actually, with that meager amount of equipment I was able to capture and document a lot. You can too!

There are many fancy gadgets used for paranormal investigations. A person can really get lost in all of the devices, capabilities and limitations of each, and go broke trying to keep up with all of the new stuff that seems to come out every full moon. Internet stores that sell paranormal investigating paraphernalia make good money hyping up equipment – that is their business and how they have decided to make a living, so more power to them. Nevertheless, the reality is that there are few things that you really **NEED**.

Here is a short list of things that you really need to conduct a paranormal investigation:

1. A decent water supply – you must remain hydrated.
2. Good health – nothing else matters if you're not in good health.
3. A clear mind – you must be well rested and you should never attempt to investigate when even slightly impaired.
4. A good first aid kit and knowledge of first aid.
5. A working cell phone or having a phone nearby.
6. An understanding of the investigation location and emergency services nearby.
7. A working flashlight and some extra batteries.
8. Clothing suitable for the environment that you will be working in.
9. A reliable vehicle to get you to and from the investigation.

The human body, and you should have one somewhere, is a great investigative tool! It can pick up objects, sights, sounds, smells, sense temperature, and pressure. It can also be sensitive to electronic and magnetic fields. For the most part, it is a highly sensitive, multi-capable, ghost-hunting tool! The only drawback is that it does not document the experiences very well for distribution. Trying to relate an event that an investigator personally experiences with his or her body is not documented evidence. Sadly, what the person felt, heard, or saw often falls into the ghost story category to the listener. For that reason, certain devices are used that accurately measure or simply record the events that you consider paranormal. Photographs, video, instrumentation readings, and audio recordings provide the viewer with tangible evidence to make an informed opinion on what you experienced.

Regardless of how many bells, whistles, tones, or shiny light blips a device has, its primary function is to measure or document a specific event or occurrence (or combination) that will allow for sharing the measured or documented event with others. When you combine a specific measurement or documented piece of video and a personal experience, it becomes a powerful piece of evidence of a particular situation. It is no longer just a ghost story but something much more compelling. For instance, when an investigator reports that when she entered a particular room and the hair on the back of her neck stood up and the electro-magnetic field detector immediately spiked to 20 milligauss (fun fact: magnetic fields are measured in units called milligauss and abbreviated as mG), the event is now measurable, and might take on more meaning. It is the meaning of what that particular measurement indicates that is highly subjective, but the actual measurement remains the same. Because of the specificity of the measurement, there is little doubt that something caused that reading, and we know just how much. However, in this instance, the first indication was that the investigator felt something change with one or more of his/her senses.

Here are the major senses of the human body that are commonly used on investigations and their investigative device counterparts:

Physical Sense	**Devices that Mimic the Physical Senses**
Sight	Still photo cameras (digital or film), video (infrared, full-spectrum, thermal imaging, and visible light cameras).
Hearing	Audio recording devices (digital or analog)
Touch	Thermometers (digital or analog), barometers, psychrometers, EMF detectors, etc.

(Note: Taste and smell are not listed as there is not a realistic device used for ghost hunting that detects or records these senses. Most likely, ghosts probably taste much like they would smell.)

When you do decide to purchase some paranormal investigative equipment, I recommend that you only get what you think would be beneficial to the type of investigations you are able to conduct. If a client who is hearing strange noises or voices in his or her location contacts you, then obviously you might want to get a device that will record audio. If the issue involves odd shadows, apparitions, objects moving about on their own, then some type of photographic or video equipment would be appropriate to document the event(s). If the reported activity is a feeling that there are unseen forces walking around the location, then you might want to use EMF meters, geophones, motion detectors, or static field detectors. The bottom line is: get what you think you need to document the event. Trust me; you'll build up your paranormal investigative equipment arsenal sooner than you think.

The equipment that I will present in this chapter will not make you an expert on any of them. I am simply giving you some general information on the standard equipment and my personal observations and opinions regarding them. When it comes to purchasing equipment, it pays to do your homework with regard to price, reliability, as well as capabilities.

Audio-Recording Devices

One of the least expensive devices on the market is the digital audio recorder. The price range goes from fairly inexpensive to very expensive. Digital vs. Analog (tape recorders): A tape recorder has a motor in them that makes noise, solid-state digital does not. Tape recorders record sounds differently than digital. Though I prefer using digital recorder, you might increase your chances of recording something if you have at least one analog "old-school" magnetic tape device. If you do use a tape recorder in your arsenal of audio equipment, I recommend using an external microphone instead of the condenser microphone that is usually built in. This will reduce or eliminate the tape motor noise considerably. When choosing a digital recording device, I recommend that you consider these factors:

1. A good digital recorder should have enough internal memory to capture at least 8 hours of audio in a high quality mode setting.

2. It should have a headphone jack, a built-in unidirectional microphone, and a microphone jack (should you want to use it with an external or parabolic microphone).

3. It should have a USB port (so you can export your files and analyze the audio using audio analyzing and editing software).

4. It should be capable of capturing 75-20,000Hz (20KHz being the upper limit of human hearing). Human voices range from about 83-256Hz, so the recommended frequency range is capable for capturing much more than EVP data. Frequencies lower than 75Hz start to approach vibrations that are felt more than they are heard.

5. It should be battery operated and require batteries that are readily available in stores. You may elect to use rechargeable batteries for your equipment, however, I advise you to bring extras on any investigation. Battery drains occur quite often and having fully charged spares on hand is necessary.

Having a digital audio recorder is good, but having good audio-editing software to go with it is even better! This will allow you to view the waveform of your clip, thus help you decipher sounds and give you a heads-up when a loud noise is approaching in the audio clip. Good audio-editing software will allow you to copy certain segments of your original recording into smaller clips for sharing and further analysis, clean up your recording by removing background noise, isolating frequencies to help determine what that interesting sound or voice might be, and give you a means to raise the volume of the clip. You can of course go too far with your editing too, so use some restraint. If you tamper with a file of a frog croaking enough, you can create the sound of human speech so the idea is to clean up your evidence, not create new evidence. Some great software available is not too expensive, so do your research, and find one that is user friendly for non-sound engineers and does not require two limbs to purchase. In addition, there are free and low cost software titles available and I suggest that you try these out before you spend big bucks on audio analysis software. Some low-cost software titles that I am aware of are EVP maker 2.5, Audacity, and Goldwave.

Though they do not fall in the audio-recording device category, I would like to discuss other audio devices commonly called "Spirit Boxes." Some of these devices scan through radio frequencies at specified rates producing words and sounds from within the white noise, while others simply produce words via sound and/or text. The general theory behind these devices is that spirits are able to manipulate the general frequencies or energies that constantly surround us and are able to communicate through these devices. I have personally witnessed some interesting interactions with these types of devices. However, I have also witnessed some gross misuse, miscalculations, and misunderstanding of the output (see apophenia).

<u>Photographic Equipment and Video</u>
If you already own a decent camera, one that will take pictures in low lighting conditions, you might not need anything else. When someone sees a "ghost" and is disturbed enough by it to contact a paranormal team to investigate, they probably just saw it with their eyes, so a standard camera might be enough for you to document something. Most paranormal teams take still photos of the location, and even if the large volume of photos does not capture any paranormal activity, they can still be used as a reference for tying evidence gathered to a specific area.

Digital vs. Film: Both capture light thus giving you a visual image. Film cameras capture that light and the film is processed chemically, which might alter or enhance the reproduction of the original image. Before digital cameras were even thought of, film was the primary means of taking photos, and they served that purpose very well. Both types of cameras have their advantages. If you can, use both.

Video is a great tool for investigating, because it will capture movement that might be meaningful in later review. When it comes to video equipment, you might be considering some expensive equipment for purchase. If the amount of money is a consideration for you, perhaps used equipment might be an option. Whether you use a hand-held video camera or DVR surveillance set up, or a combination of both, is completely up to you. Of course, the more area you cover on an investigation using photographic or video cameras, the greater chance you have of capturing some useful data. Some recommendations for video equipment:

1. Having the ability to shoot video in the dark using infrared or full spectrum (IR + UV + visible lighting) might allow you to capture the seen and unseen to the human eye. A hand-held video camera with night vision might prevent you from falling down unseen stairs while you are stumbling around in the dark.

2. Handheld cameras should be used that record on memory sticks or an internal hard disk. Using a video camera that requires tapes or blank DVDs make noise. Remember, you are recording audio with your handheld video too, so the quieter your device is the better!

3. Multi-channel DVR surveillance systems are really nice to have. You can generally record many hours of data, review the data on the fly, and output the data for video analysis and transfer. The cameras that you connect to the DVR system can be IR or Full Spectrum, or a combination. A 4 camera system might be enough for you, and it is not too terribly expensive.

4. Just like the audio software, you might consider some video-editing software for analysis and sharing of your video data/evidence. Software that will allow you to create clips of the video of interest, raise the brightness or contrast, or enhance the quality of the recording is very useful. Do your homework on the purchase of video-editing software though; some of them can be very expensive and not any more useful to you than less expensive software products.

Thermometers, Barometers, Psychrometers, and Atmospheric Equipment

Of all of these devices, a good probe thermometer is a good tool to have. An instant-read probe thermometer is even better, especially when you locate a "cold spot." By using a probe thermometer you can almost trace and outline the cold spot as if it were a solid object. There are also instant-read laser thermometers, but they require the laser to bounce off of a surface to give you the surface temperature of an object (which is nice, but it will not give you a specific reading for a chunk of air in the middle of the room that is a different temperature than the rest of the room).

Barometers measure pressure changes in the atmosphere, and though they can be an investigative tool, they are rarely used. The same goes for psychrometers (measuring dew point) and other atmospheric equipment (measuring amounts of specific gases in a space; carbon monoxide, dioxide, etc.). In an investigation where the client is reporting that people get headaches, dizziness, nausea, or even pass out in a certain location, it might be best to recommend that they have the area checked for noxious gases BEFORE you put yourself or your team in jeopardy.

Electro-Magnetic Field Detectors

There are many EMF detectors for sale, and for good reason. Long exposure to EMF radiation can cause health risks, and if the EMF levels are high enough, it can cause immediate effects to someone that is sensitive to them (light-headedness, anxiety, and hallucinations have been reportedly associated with high EMF levels). The two main types of EMF are AC and DC. AC is normally associated with man-made electricity and electrical components; DC with battery and naturally occurring magnetic fields. The lower-priced EMF meters will measure in one axis (so you have to move it around to get readings in the other two) but the moderate to expensive EMF detectors will measure all 3 axes simultaneously. My recommendation, if you decide to get one, is to choose one that measures as many things as possible (magnetic, electric, and radio/microwave) in all axes.

Motion Detectors

There are many motion detectors available. These can be very helpful for detecting movement in a space where none of your team members are. You can purchase them at various specialty stores, but I highly recommend comparing prices at your local hardware chains first. Some have audible alarms and some light up, which may affect your other equipment in a space. I always try to get the most "bang for my buck," so I always look around and see if I can find some reviews first.

Metaphysical Ghost-Hunting Equipment

This category of equipment includes dowsing rods, pendulums, crystals, communication boards, etc. I personally neither endorse nor condemn the use of these tools for ghost hunting. Though most of these tools alone are not able to document a paranormal experience, using these in conjunction with video or audio equipment possibly could. There is a lot of controversy within the paranormal community regarding the use of some of these tools, especially in the case of the Ouija board: many people say that if you use it to communicate with spirits, you open up a doorway and suffer negative and generally nasty consequences. In my opinion, if that is true, then we do that every time we conduct and EVP session during an investigation; we are still inviting communication, just using different equipment. This is a field where success is determined by results; believing that you will get results by using metaphysical tools during investigations is entirely up to you. Keep in mind that your clients might also have strong beliefs regarding such tools, and you need to be very mindful of their concerns.

Other Investigative Gizmos

There are many new gadgets coming out all the time. Read the reviews of them, and see if they will be useful on your investigations. If anything, they might be fun to play with, and prove useful on investigations. Keep in mind that most equipment that paranormal investigators use was not originally designed for ghost hunting. The EMF detectors, temperature sensing devices, and audio/video recording equipment were originally designed for much different purposes other than what you will use them for. You might discover a new use of a commonplace piece of equipment that might prove vital in future investigations. Who would have thought that the everyday hair dryer put off so much EMF that it attracted ghosts?

Having provided a very superficial outline of different investigative equipment in this chapter, I thought it might be helpful to give you some idea of what equipment might be good for an emerging paranormal team. This array of equipment would allow for proper documentation of common occurrences found on paranormal investigations:

A 4-camera IR DVR system with a light-weight portable monitor, a 5 megapixel digital camera (or better), a digital audio recorder for each DVR camera and 2 additional (6 total), a Tri-Field EMF meter, a probe thermometer, a bubble level*, and 4 walkie-talkies of good quality. Do not forget to add a durable coffee maker to the list.

* A bubble level is a great tool for investigations. Un-level floors or walls can explain odd feelings in certain rooms. A bubble level can help determine if you are experiencing a "fun house" effect or if there might be another cause for unusual feelings.

4 PREPARING FOR A PARANORMAL INVESTIGATION

Proper preparation is probably the most important thing that you do as a paranormal investigator. Without it, your investigation will most likely represent a colossal waste of time for you and your team. When you are new to the field, it is hard to know where to start, much less to have a clear idea of what proper preparation is. This chapter will give you some suggestions and a general description of what the preparation animal looks like.

<u>Research</u>

People are going to contact you if you publicize your services. Some of those people are legitimately going to be asking for your help, some just want someone non-judgmental to talk about their experiences, and some people (to say this nicely) should really contact some type of health professional instead.

When first contacted by a client who is experiencing what the client believes is paranormal activity, you are going to be excited. It would be great to don your jumpsuit, strap on your proton packs, and jump into Ecto 1 with a crazy siren wailing as you rush to save the paranormal day! But that hardly ever happens. Before you start recharging the batteries in all your equipment, you need to do some research.

The first thing you should examine is the property owner. Whether a property owner asks you and your team to look into the activity that is occurring in their home or business, or you received permission to investigate a location on your request, looking into the property owner can save you many problems later on. This is especially true when you are contacted by someone to investigate that is renting the location. Remember: the people that contact you have specific motivations for doing so, and sometimes those motivations are not on the up and up.

(Note: This handbook is not written by a law professional. It is HIGHLY recommended that you talk to one before you start investigating. You may see this statement more than once.)

One of your first steps would be to conduct an interview, preferably at the location. Have the property owner complete a client questionnaire (an example of such a form is supplied in the useful forms chapter), and do your best when interviewing them to determine if they are being genuine. When you go to the location for an interview, do not go alone, have someone, ideally a team member, go with you. If at any time you feel unsafe, even if that feeling hits you before you walk in for the interview, leave. If you enter the location and you see any evidence of illegal activity or obvious unsafe conditions; leave. Should the owners seem genuine and the location seem safe for an investigation, thank the owner and let them know that you'll be in touch with them soon to discuss investigation options.

After you receive the completed questionnaire, you should have enough information to start doing some research on the location owner. You may simply put their name, email address, phone number, or location address in an Internet search, and start from there. Criminal activity associated with any of the above searches should be enough to stop any attempts for setting up an investigation. For instance, if you find out that the owner has a few legal proceedings filed against workers or contractors that have entered the location, you might consider that you and your team are being set up for a legal battle you might not be prepared for. Alternatively, you might learn that the location has a history of criminal activity, legal action against the property owners, or something out of the ordinary that just does not sound like it is on the up and up. Do not put yourself or your team at risk, just pass on this one.

If the owners of the property check out without any startling discoveries, start researching the property. The Internet, city hall, or a local historian might give you some background on the location and its history. You might also want to look at a topographical map (a satellite-view map is great too). Knowing the elevation, ground type, vicinity of high power lines, sewer locations, septic drainage, microwave towers, etc., might be important to explain some of the paranormal claims at the location. This is also a good time to discover what emergency and other services are near the location should you take this case.

Having investigated the owner and location, you should have written down all of your findings or lack of findings. These findings can be included in your final report of your investigation should you decide to conduct one. You are now ready to begin preparing for an investigation.

Investigative Preparations

Before you start calling or emailing your team, look over the questionnaire completed by the client. What is the size of the location? What type of activity is occurring? When is the activity happening? Answering these questions will help you decide how many team members you will want to bring with you and which team members might possess the right qualities, what equipment would be best to document or debunk the claims, and what time would increase your chances of getting possible evidence. Now you can coordinate with the owner(s) and your team, and set up the investigation date and time.

With an investigation date set up, start going over the equipment that you will bring with you, and be sure it is all in good condition. Make a small inventory sheet of the equipment that you will bring with you (this will also be helpful when breaking down from the investigation). There is nothing worse than arriving to a location and finding out that a piece of equipment that you were counting on does not work, or leaving an investigation and forgetting a piece of your equipment. Some of those technical doodads are expensive!

The day before the investigation, double check the batteries in any equipment that you will depend on, and make sure you pack extras. Go through your first aid kit and see if it will meet the needs of potential problems you might run into (are poisonous critters lurking about at the site?). If you noted the presence of high- dust concentrations or mold, bringing some dust masks and some rubber gloves never hurt. You and your team's safety is much more important than getting evidence of ghosts, Bigfoot, extraterrestrials, werewolves, or whatever oddity you have planned to capture.

When you feel that you have everything prepared, discuss your preparations with your team. Someone always has a great idea for something to add to the list, so listen to him or her. A team works best when everyone has an input. A meeting before the investigation will help you devise an overall plan that will make the investigation efficient. Without a plan, you and your team will be aimlessly walking around, asking the same dumb questions, and not accomplish much if anything.

The Investigation Plan

Before you and your team start running around the location setting up equipment and forming investigative groups, you need to have a plan. Without an investigative plan, you and your team will be aimlessly running around the location looking like a lost episode of *Scooby Doo*. Creating an investigative plan dictates your and your team's actions throughout the investigation, and can make the experience meaningful.

This plan can be formal or informal, and either can be just as effective. A formal plan might be written and include diagrams or blueprints of the location. Having a formal plan might be a good idea when you first start investigating, because you can refer back to it, learn what worked and what did not work, where key equipment was placed, etc. An informal plan might be just a verbal understanding with all of the investigators. Your method is entirely up to you, but please remember: if you are going into this field with the hopes of gathering scientific evidence of whatever it is that you are trying to prove or disprove, you might always want to use a formal plan. If all of your evidence and your investigative plan can stand up to scrutiny, you and your team have done your job.

The first step in creating an investigation plan is to have an investigative goal. What do you intend to achieve or accomplish on this particular investigation? Is your goal to prove or disprove the client's claims of paranormal activity in the home? Are you trying to prove or disprove the claims of paranormal activity in a location that is popularly thought to have activity? Whatever the reason of why you are involved with the particular location will most likely steer you toward the goal of having an investigation. It certainly makes sense to involve the client in establishing this goal. With the client involved in the setting of the goal, you will ensure that you meet the needs of the client, establish focus for you and your team's investigation, and that the time you spend conducting the investigation remains purposeful.

Once you have established the investigative goal, you need to plan on how you will accomplish it. How many people will you need? What type of equipment would be necessary or useful? How long should it take? All of these questions should be addressed in your plan. If particular events are occurring in specific areas of the location, draw a diagram and annotate where you will strategically place equipment.

Other considerations for your plan might include the number of investigators in the location at a time, availability of electrical power, and the time of day that you will be investigating. There are certain times of day or night that are better for an investigation (because of sound, light, or reports of activity) and those factors vary with each location and situation. The more thorough your plan is the better! A thorough plan is not necessarily a rigid one. You must remain flexible, and alter your plan if needed. The expression, "Shit happens," was probably the result of a paranormal investigation that was planned poorly, had gone terribly wrong, or the conditions of the investigation changed drastically catching the paranormal team off-guard.

The following example plan was derived from a fictitious client questionnaire. As you may have noticed, the bottom portion of the questionnaire is specifically designed to form an investigation plan. This plan focuses on the reports of paranormal activity experienced by a homeowner in a small home. (Note: The questionnaire is abbreviated to target the activity for which the sample investigation will concentrate.)

Questionnaire and Investigation Plan (Example)

Client Information

Name of Client	Resident of address?	X	Yes
Cecil Andbeanie			No

Phone Number with Area Code	Email Address
(360) 555-5555	beanie@whatever.com

Interview

Case Number:	2011-11	Date of contact:	27 March 2011
Case Interviewer:	Michael	Date of Interview:	3 April 2011
Interview Location:	Residence	Time of Interview:	5:30PM

Location Information

Street Address			City, State		
1438 Elmwood Tree Lane			Anytown, WA		
Nature of residence:	X	Home	Client own or rent the residence?	X	Own
		Apartment			Rent
		Other (explain):			

Nature of Paranormal Activity (Brief description of what is occurring)

Voices are heard in the kitchen at various times, mostly at night. Physical contact in kitchen and hallway. Feelings of being watched in kitchen.

Specific Activity

Auditory Events (Explain in details)		Details
X	Voices	Whispering voices in the kitchen most often heard while everyone is trying to sleep. Sounds like a man and a woman talking. No discernible words or names.
	Calling of a name(s)	
	Footsteps	
	Strange sounds or growling	
	Tapping or knocking	
	Conversations with spirit(s)	
	Other	

Physical Events (Explain in details)		Details
X	Being touched, shoved, or grabbed	6 year-old son has reported feeling like his hair was being touched or patted on the head.
	Tugging on clothing	
	Hair on arms or neck standing on end	
	Hot or cold spots	
	Objects moving without apparent cause	
	Unexplained odors	
	Appliances turning on or off	
	Doors or windows opening/closing	
	Other	

Emotional Events(Explain in details)		Details
	Intense random thoughts	Dining area is attached to the kitchen. When the family is eating, they have feelings of being watched.
X	Feeling of being watched or followed	
	Mood changes (especially in one room)	
	Unexplained stress or anxiety	
	Unexplained feelings of joy or anger	
	Recent anniversary of a significant event	
	Other	

Resident Information (List all occupants residing at the residence)

Name	Age			Religion	Yrs lived at address
		X	Male	Religion	7
Cecil Andbeanie	36		Female	None	
Name	Age		Male	Religion None- Catholic	Yrs lived at address
					7
Polly Andbeanie	34	X	Female		
Name	Age	X	Male	Religion	Yrs lived at address
					6
William Andbeanie	6		Female	None	

Investigation Plan

1. Attach a drawing or map of the residence to the back of this form. Mark areas to show known paranormal activity.		
2. What would be the goal of a paranormal investigation?		To document activity and identify who or what may be talking/whispering/touching. If it is an entity or entities, find out what they want.
3. Are there any off-limits areas in the residence or on the property that you do not want an investigative team to enter?		Yes	If Yes, what area(s):
	X	No	
4. Do you know of any health or safety issues that might present a danger to an investigative team?		Yes	If Yes, explain:
	X	No	

5. Are there any special concerns that you have regarding a possible investigation of the residence?	X	Yes	If Yes, explain:
		No	Would like to be discrete because of nosey neighbors. Would prefer if any documentation or evidence received on the investigation does not mention family name or address.
6. Other considerations?		Yes	If Yes, explain:
	X	No	

Investigation				
Scheduled for:	10 March 2011	Time:	7:30 - 11:30 PM
Assigned Investigators:		Michael	
		Kathy	
		Mark	
		Alex	
		Colleen	

Equipment to accomplish goal: Digital recorders, EMF meters, DVR IR cameras.

Overall plan: Cover all areas with reported activity with DVR cameras and digital audio recorders. Investigators will conduct EVP sessions in pairs with only one pair in the residence at any given time. EMF sweep of entire house will be conducted. Base station will be manned by remaining members. Residents of the household will remain at base for the duration of the investigation, so no emergency contact numbers are needed.

DVR IR Camera setup: Kitchen, dining room, hallway, and entryway. Refer to diagram - arrows indicate IR camera and angle. Digital audio recorders: Near each IR camera.

EVP questions:
Who are you? (Use variations to attempt to get a solid identification.)
What is your name? (Each team should try this direct question.)
Do you have a connection to the family that lives here? (Avoid questions that might provide a negative answer, i.e. "Do you like the people that live here?")
Why are you here? (Use variations)

Diagram:

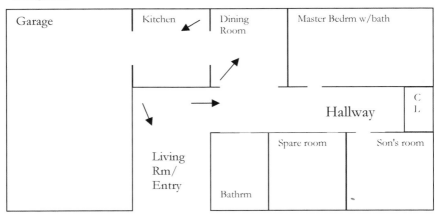

(One small note with regard to the scenario above: with experience you will have some suspicions with the reported locations and types of activity. Those feelings are valid if they do not create a bias in the investigative process.)

Summary

By creating a plan, the investigation now has purpose. The client's concerns regarding the activity are addressed by the investigation, and you have placed your equipment in the best possible areas to potentially capture some data. Now that you have a plan and you have reviewed your plan with your team, it is time to start an investigation!

5 PERCEPTION ERRORS

I know that you are anxious to get into this location and start investigating. I fully understand your excitement, but I think we should talk a little bit first. You see, there is this little thing called "perception" that is going to influence every single thing that you see and hear during your investigation, and it warrants some discussion.

When I was planning this book, I devoted a chapter to perception errors during and on post review of a paranormal investigation. Then I took it out of the book entirely. Then, I placed it as a note in the chapter about conducting an investigation. When I got to the third page of the draft, I realized that this cannot be just a note in a chapter, and put it right back here where I planned it to be. The more I thought about it, the more I realized that the subject deserves more than one chapter; in fact, it deserves its own book! Rather than directing you to another book to read, I thought I would give you enough to think about regarding the impact of your own perceptions during your investigation. I hope that this will reduce the inevitable perception errors that will be present during and after your investigation.

"Your eyes can deceive you, don't trust them." - Obi Wan Kenobi. No truer words have ever been spoken in a movie. If old Obi Wan had been a paranormal investigator, he would have added that your ears will deceive you even more!

Have you ever seen or heard something that surprised you? The event that surprised you might not have been anything too out of the ordinary; in fact, it might have been downright mundane. The reason it surprised you was that it fell outside of your expectations. In other words, it presented a reality that was not the same as the one you had established, and therefore caught you off-guard.

Now brace yourself! I am going to throw some terms into your brain, and I hope that they are not too painfully received. I know this might not be pleasant, but it cannot be helped. I could avoid the subject entirely, but I think that would be cheating you out of some objectivity, and objectivity is the most important quality of any investigation. So without further delay, here come the terms!

The first term is "apophenia." Apophenia is the psychological tendency to derive meaning from otherwise random events. A type of apophenia is pareidolia, which can be from visual or auditory stimuli. Examples of pareidolia would be seeing the face on Mars, animals or other objects in cloud formations, the Man on the Moon, or hearing "secret messages" in audio recordings. These are natural tendencies as people attempt to understand and give meaning to the data that they receive from the world around them.

What we see and what we hear are simply our perceptions of what we see and hear. Quite often, our perceptions of the world around us differ from the world that gave us the stimuli. These differences during an investigation can be considered perception errors at times. As paranormal investigators, we need to be conscious of these errors in perception while we are conducting our investigations and during post-review.

At some point in your life, someone has probably said, "Perception is everything." Chances are you may have said this yourself more than once. This is a very true statement! Our perceptions define our reality. To say that all of our perceptions are based on factual or actual data would be an exaggeration of the truth. As human beings, we are subject to errors in perception. As paranormal investigators, these errors can skew our data to the point that objectivity is placed in jeopardy. In order to reduce these errors, we must understand where these errors come from.

Perception errors arise from the mind's attempt to process and understand the data that it is receiving. Unlike our digital audio recorders and various cameras that simply record the events, our mind interprets the data, and, at times, assigns meaning to it based on factors derived from events outside of the initially received data. For the purpose of understanding, the descriptions below will concentrate on the perception of sound even though what we see is influenced almost, if not just, as much.

When a person hears a sound, it passes through the unimpaired ear and sends a signal to the brain. So far, this is purely a mechanical operation, and the errors that I will illustrate have not been introduced yet. Errors are introduced when the mind filters the sound input in order to understand it. Think of this like a set of mental filters; once the sound has passed through all of these filters, it is now called the perceived sound. The perceived sound may be similar to or vastly different from the original sound source.

The first filter that is engaged is memory. An instantaneous question is asked within the mind, "Has this sound been heard before?" It is almost like searching through a file cabinet. This is an identification process, because if this sound had been heard before, the filter tries to identify it as a known source. If the sound is new, then this filter tries to find something that sounded similar before.

Another filter deals with beliefs and expectations. Beliefs, religious and/ or spiritual, and beliefs founded in the world, as you perceive them, have a major impact on your perceived sounds. If your belief system is unshakable, whatever you see and hear will be altered. If you believe without a shadow of doubt that the location you are going to is haunted by demons, most of what you see, hear, or encounter will be of a demonic nature. It is just like wearing blue sunglasses; everything you see will have a blue tint.

The filter of fear and anxiety is multi-faceted. This filter covers everything from fear of the boogieman to the anxiety of leaving the iron on at home while you are out investigating. The physiological effects of fear can affect all other senses and bodily functions. If you let fear dominate you, your investigation will seriously lack objectivity and probably will not be too enjoyable. When this filter is fully engaged, every sight and sound takes on a different meaning. That ruffle in your clothing that irons itself out due to gravity suddenly becomes a tug from an unseen entity. That creek from the house settling is now perceived as a voice.

The last filter I would like to propose is the filter of assumption. This is an associative error that virtually all paranormal investigators are subject to. Hearing a bell ring on an investigation might not have any special meaning, but hearing a bell ring when you are investigating the lobby of an abandoned hotel can take on new meaning based on assumptions of what goes on at a hotel. People that are highly suggestible are very prone to making associative errors.

These filters act independently, in combination, and sometimes all together to orchestrate a symphony of errors that present a perceived reality that can be vastly different from the existing environmental factors. When these filters orchestrate a symphony of perceived reality, it is a marvel to behold: a series of random events linked together form a pattern that might be associated with paranormal activity (see apophenia). Here is an example of this orchestra in action:

A team is contacted by a client to investigate a household that has been experiencing unexplained voices coming from various locations throughout the house. Additionally, toys move and mysteriously turn on in their child's bedroom; their cat, who was calm in their previous residence is now always on edge; footsteps and the sound of running has been heard in the basement; and the light in the bathroom turns on in the middle of the night. The history of this house revolves around a little girl who died by falling down the basement stairs.

During an investigation of this location in the basement, one of the investigators, completely familiar with the history and reports, hears a sound, and the mental filters kick in setting off a chain reaction. The sound enters the ear and is transferred to the brain. The mind filters this sound with memory remembering what a little girl's voice sounds like. Belief in the spirit of the little girl at that location amplifies the expectation of hearing a little girl's voice. Because this basement is completely in the dark, it seems very creepy and dangerous, and sounds are amplified due to a heightened state of awareness. Reports have indicated that there were voices present and a little girl passed away in the basement, so the investigator assumes the sound that he heard belonged to the little girl. Because this filtering has altered the perception of the existing environmental conditions, the cat, that was quietly hiding underneath the stairs farts, and it results in the investigator turning to his partner with wide-eyed surprise, "That's that little girl!"

Now, please do not get me wrong. I am not saying that everything that we hear or see on an investigation is simply an error in perception or a psychological manifestation. In fact, it is remotely possible, however unlikely, that the little girl in the example above was trying to communicate through feline flatulence! There are events that just cannot be explained away that would suggest that paranormal activity is indeed occurring in a location. What I am presenting here is an opportunity to understand that perception errors exist, how to recognize them in action, and how to reduce their impact so that your investigation becomes an objective and rational activity.

To significantly reduce possible perception errors there are steps that you can take. You know yourself better than anyone else does, so these steps might be more than you need to conduct an objective investigation. Then again, perhaps you may have thought of some additional steps that would work best for you or others. These are but a few suggestions to reduce perception errors:

Ground yourself. Take a few moments before you start your investigation, and breathe deeply. Let the worries and concerns of the past and the future slip away. Become present with the here and now and let nothing else enter your mind.

Sample the environment. When the lights are on, walk through the location, and pay particular attention to where all of the shadows naturally fall, where pictures or paintings of people are, how objects in the corners and behind doors appear from a direct view and from the corner of your eye. Listen to the sounds of the floors as you walk on them, open and close doors to see if they creak, listen to the natural sounds of the structure and outside noises. Take notes.

Use a trusted agent. A trusted agent on the team knows the history of the location, the details and reports of activity, as well as the names that have been associated with the reports of paranormal activity. Instead of letting every team member know that a little girl named Lilly had died by falling down the stairs that led to the basement and that reports of a little girl's voice had been heard in that area, only let one or two people know that information. Team members can be told that they may be able to get audio or video evidence in specific areas of interest so they can place the appropriate equipment in those spaces. It would make sense that the person who conducted the original interview with the client is the, or one of your trusted agents.

Avoid suggestibility. Instead of asking your investigative partner, "Did you hear that voice say, 'Get out?!'" ask, "Did you hear something?" then both of you may write down what you had heard. Later, give your notes to an objective third party who can compare them. A suggestible person might honestly believe, convincing themselves, that they heard exactly what you had heard, when in fact there is doubt that they heard anything at all.

Focus on the sight or sound. Accept the sounds you hear and the sights you see as they are without associating them with something else. When you hear that bell in the abandoned hotel lobby, concentrate on the actual sound itself, not the fact that it sounded like a bell calling a bellhop.

Now that you are aware that these errors exist, and you know how to reduce their impact, you may now investigate more objectively. Now, off to the investigation with you!

6 CONDUCTING AN INVESTIGATION

The investigation itself is what most paranormal investigators look forward to because it is usually interesting and fun! It is also a very serious undertaking, and requires concentration by all team members. This event defines what you and your team are capable of. If you conduct your investigation professionally and thoughtfully, you will come up with better results, and your team's reputation will earn you respect, which will result in more investigations coming your way.

No doubt, your first investigation is going to create some anxiety, as well as excitement. The word 'fear' might even come into play. There are many theories, superstitions, and beliefs regarding paranormal activity and none of them are without their merits. Keep in mind that you are there to perform a job; your job is to gather information regarding the reports of paranormal activity. Just like any job, you might not perform very well initially, or you might find out that you or your team is not mentally or physically prepared for what you might find. If you always keep your and your team's safety as the number one priority, you should do fine. Never be ashamed to turn over an investigation to a more experienced team that might be better prepared for it. Remember, it is about obtaining evidence of paranormal activity, not padding your ego.

<u>Pre-Arrival</u>
Before you leave the safety and security of your home, take a few minutes to double-check your inventory of equipment and supplies. Having some tools, electrical tape, painters tape (for taping down cords), trash bag, hand cleaner, and perhaps a folding chair or two might come in handy. Check the weather report for the investigation area, and make sure that you are dressing appropriately for the existing and future conditions. I know I might be

sounding like your mom here, but believe me: you cannot conduct a good investigation if you are not dressed for the conditions. Regarding your clothing, it should be non-reflective (black cloth is best) and fit snuggly. You should not have any loops or excess material hanging loosely. In addition, you should restrict the amount of jewelry that you wear as it may snag on something, make noise, and possibly affect the readings on your instruments. If you are one of those people that measures your success in life by how many keys you have hanging off your belt, take a day off from that.

Just a word about wearing cologne or perfume, and use of scented soaps the day of an investigation: Do not use them. Sure, the commercials show the use of the products causing members of the opposite sex going nuts over the wearer; I am sorry to inform you that this scenario is fiction, and does not occur in real life. In real life, some people are very sensitive to these scented products; this can include your teammates and your clients. I am not suggesting that ghosts are sensitive to these fragrances, but, if you are in an abandoned building that used to be a brothel, you might not be able to pick up that faint smell of perfume or roses that might indicate that you are not alone if your body spray is overpowering.

Arrival

How you conduct yourself upon arrival will determine how the rest of the evening goes. Before you start unpacking all of your equipment, meet with the client and introduce your team. It is important that the client feels comfortable with you and your team being on their premises. If they do not trust you because of how your team is behaving or how respectful your team is to the client and the property, they might not want you to conduct the investigation, or they might not be as open about the experiences that you want them to convey. Do not think for a moment that just because you all are wearing a paranormal team logo on your clothing that people trust that you know what you are doing. If you and your team are intently listening to the client, understand the client's concerns regarding the investigation, and remain respectful, you have just jumped the first hurdle in a series of hurdles that are ahead.

(This is an important note: If during the walkabout with the client you see evidence of criminal activity on the property, leave. There is no sense conducting an investigation that might implicate you or your team in a criminal investigation later on. Whether you simply leave, or leave and notify the proper authorities is up to you; the important thing is to get your team out of there!)

While walking around with the client, it is important to make note of the objects and obstructions that might present a safety hazard. That Ming Dynasty vase at the top of the staircase sure looks pretty, but when you and your team are walking around the house in the dark, that same vase might not be so pretty in ten thousand twinkling pieces adorning the stairs. You should suggest that the client remove it before the investigation starts. Those weak spots in the floor of the attic, that one electrical outlet that occasionally vomits some sparks, that basket of decorative sharp sticks on the coffee table, are all items that should warrant your team's attention. If a safety hazard or something fragile is visible when the lights are on, it is a bigger safety hazard and twice as fragile when the lights are off. Move these items out of the way or clearly mark a perimeter around them.

After the client has met the team, has shown the location to everyone, and addressed his or her concerns, it is time for you to discuss your investigative plan. If the client and your team all seem to think that it is a good plan, then it is time to get some paperwork signed that will:

1. Give you permission to investigate. Without written permission, you really are skating on thin ice. This is especially true if the owner is not going to be present during your investigation. You run the risk of being detained for trespassing, or worse. Only the owner can give you written permission to conduct your investigation, so you need to be sure that the client owns the establishment. If the client is only renting the space, their permission might not be enough should an adverse condition arise.

2. Establish some liability ground rules. Who is going to be responsible should someone get hurt, accidentally break something, cause a fire, or any other adverse condition arising from your investigation there? You need to have some kind of agreement in writing.

3. Review the confidentiality agreement of the investigation with the owner and all of your investigation team (including the owner, employees of the establishment, or occupants of the location if they are to accompany the investigative team). The Confidentiality Agreement states that the investigative team: "will protect the confidentiality of all pertinent information, including specific location details, specifics of the paranormal activity, personal information about the client, and any other information that is asked to be kept confidential.

By signing this form, we agree to hold all evidence (photographic, video and audio) we capture during this investigation in the strictest of confidence, and shall not share said evidence with the public or any other paranormal group unless given permission to do otherwise."

(NOTE: As a reminder, this handbook is not written by a law professional! You should speak with one BEFORE you begin investigating. Present your general forms to a law professional and get their feedback, or commission their services in creating some forms for your team. The money you will spend with a legal professional will save you several times that if a lawsuit arises from something that occurred during one of your investigations.)

<u>Setup</u>

If you had a good investigative plan that outlined where all of your equipment is going to be placed, setup is a very easy step! If during your walkabout with the client you believe that you should alter your plan, make sure that all team members are aware of it. Your team needs to be a chorus all singing from the same sheet music.

1. Establish an isolated area, and call it base. Your base is especially important if you are using a DVR camera system. This is one of the most important areas of the investigation even though many people do not find it the most exciting area. The base station is where you will monitor and control everything that goes on during the investigative event. Ideally, this area should: Have your DVR monitor and a person stationed there at all times keeping a log, hold all of your ancillary equipment, be the main communications center, have your first aid kit and whatever else you brought with you (especially the most important item on a nighttime investigation - the coffee pot). This is the time that you should be running the cords to your DVR cameras and taping them down. Painter's tape is good to use for this, because the likelihood of it removing paint or wallpaper from walls is greatly reduced.

The base station log is the best tool for you to write your investigative report from. It would be a good idea that this chronological narrative is included as a part of your investigation plan. The log should note the date and location of the investigation, the time, the phase of the moon, temperature, weather information noting any significant changes, the location of all DVR cameras and digital recorders, and the location of all members as they investigate. If a team member reports a personal experience, it should be logged with who felt/heard/saw whatever it was, and the time and location of the occurrence. Anecdotal reports are not evidence, but they can be just as compelling. This log needs to be thorough enough to document everything that went on in an investigation to a point that when complete, anyone reading it could recreate the event. It is a VERY good idea to train each member on the use of base station equipment and proper log keeping.

2. Synchronize your timepieces. If you have a DVR camera setup, as most investigators do, set the time on the DVR system to the most accurate timepiece that you have with you. If you have a smart phone, you can set the DVR time to your phone. Once the DVR system time is set, it becomes your reference to everything else. All digital audio recorders should be set to the DVR time so if you capture something significant on audio or video, you can easily mate the two together and present it as a single file (more on this in the next chapter).

3. Perform a quick check on your equipment. Test your communications equipment, check your battery levels in your recorders, and see if anyone has

any concerns about the investigation before you start. Is that coffee brewing yet? You are probably going to need it at some point.

4. Before you place your digital audio recorders with each camera or in other areas designated by your plan, you need to start recording and establish a time mark. You can either start and mark it from base, or take it to its planned location and contact base for a time check. The more accurate you are with recording the time on your audio device, the more accurate your data review will be. Personally, I like starting the recording at base and performing a time mark there to the DVR system. I start the recording in the highest quality mode, announce the digital recorder number (if you are using more than one on your investigations, it would be a good idea to identify them somehow), announce the date, location, and DVR time (HOUR:MINUTES:SECONDS), and where this device is going to be placed. I would then take the device to its planned location, and once there, I set it in place and announce where it is (be as specific as possible - in the dining room in the center of the table pointing toward the kitchen).

5. Pre-investigation activities: Before you go *lights out*, this is a good time to take pictures of the location, temperature, and baseline EMF readings. Record the results of all readings because it will be important to know if there are any changes when your teams are out collecting data. Also, conduct a safety sweep of the entire location: note weak spots or gaping holes in the floor, trip hazards, fragile items, cobwebs, and any other unsafe or unhealthy items. Make sure all team members are aware of these.

Investigate

Your setup phase is over, the equipment is all up and running, and now you are ready to go *lights out* and start investigating. Honestly, this is the interesting and fun part! However, just because it is fun, it doesn't mean that it isn't a serious undertaking involving a lot of concentration, critical thinking, and strategy. The "fun" is more like playing a friendly game of chess compared to the "fun" of a water balloon fight in the dark (if you place small glow sticks in the water balloons it becomes much cooler though).

One of the first things you should do, and you will probably have to remind everyone even if they have been on a hundred investigations, is to set their cellular phone to airplane mode. This ensures that readings, especially on your EMF meters/detectors, remain valid.

1. Decide who will man the base station first, and who will investigate a particular area first. It is always good to send out people in teams of two for safety reasons. Depending on the size of the location and how sound travels, you might have only one team go to a particular area at a time. Be sure to keep your team occupied with something, or they might not perform well due to boredom. If the structure is relatively small yet you have more

investigators, consider sending a team outside to do an investigation on the grounds (quietly).

The person manning the base station has many responsibilities. This person will be monitoring the DVR display and logging everything of interest there. This person will also be keeping track of all investigative team locations, and locations of equipment that teams bring out with them, and serve as the hub of communications. The base station is also where extra team members are in standby, so it is pretty easy to fall into discussions that take away from the task at hand. The person at base needs to be able to tell other members to be quiet, or to focus their attention on the investigation tactfully. Though it is probably a less than glamorous position, manning base is probably the most important one to ensure a good investigative result.

2. Assign and deploy investigative teams. When choosing members to act as pairs, it is very important to pair them wisely. Put someone that is very talkative with someone who is less talkative and more observant; someone who is very timid or shy with someone who is a bit more confident; and someone who is technically savvy with someone who is not; and someone who is sensitive with someone who is not. Sending your team members out to investigate is a strategic maneuver, so it should be done with some thought behind it. This is a good reason of why you should really know your team well.

In the Investigation Plan example, provided in the previous chapter, you might want to send in one team to the kitchen area. As the team moves through the house, they should identify themselves as they enter each space. For example, "Mark and Kathy are entering the living room, Mark and Kathy are entering the dining room, Mark and Kathy are in the kitchen," etc. You do this so that during data review the listener knows that the rustling of clothing, the footsteps, and voices are of the team investigators and not an unknown entity.

When a team is out investigating, they need to have a heightened sense of awareness to everything going on around them. If they conduct an EVP session, the questions should have some thought behind them. In your "Investigative Plan," you should have identified some specific questions to ask.

3. After a specified time, no more than a half an hour or so, rotate your investigative teams. Have the first team report to base, provide a debrief of the EVP questions that they asked, discuss any abnormalities encountered, and then send out the next team. When the last team is making their rounds, they should make a general announcement that they are the last team, so if anyone has something to say, they should do so now. This is kind of a last call for any possible entity that wishes to communicate.

Considerations and procedures for deployed investigative teams during a paranormal investigation:

EVP Sessions: When you or your team conducts an EVP session, you should approach it as you would any other conversation with a complete stranger. Just because you ask a question and do not receive a response, it does not mean that no one is there. Imagine for a moment that you are in a crowded bus station. If you walk up to strangers and start asking them questions, chances are that they will not answer you. They might walk away, call Homeland Security because of your suspicious nature, or punch you in the head. You need to follow the same social conventions when conducting an EVP session as you would a conversation with any stranger.

1. Introduce yourself as you would to anyone before you start firing questions away. Most people do not feel comfortable speaking to a stranger, much less answering their questions. By introducing yourself, you hope to begin an exchange of information and ideas called a conversation. Try it with the living sometime, it can be fun!

2. Provide an explanation of why you are there and what you hope to gain from a conversation. This establishes a motivation to engage in a discussion. It preempts the thought that most listeners would have, "Why are you here?"

3. When asking a question, leave some time for an answer before you ask another. Have you ever had a conversation with someone that just talks and does not involve you, or leave you time to answer a question? You are not there to fire off questions; you are there to get answers.

4. Do not assume that you are speaking to one individual. One big advantage that unseen entities have, and your biggest challenge as an investigator, is that they are normally invisible. Though you may have the feeling that someone is there, you really do not know for sure who it is or how many of them are there. If the reported activity has been surrounding a little girl named Anna, do not assume that is whom you are speaking with. Ask for a name as if you were unaware of the previous reports or history of the location. If you give the answer within your question, count on the answer being the same. You would only be hearing what you expected to hear.

5. Sometimes, you can hear the answers, as well as record them. Sometimes this can be unnerving. Though hearing a direct answer from an unseen entity can be disturbing, hold your ground and remain calm. One funny thing about ghost hunting, your chance of running into one is greatly increased so you should be prepared for it.

6. Should you receive an answer to your questions, either with your own ears, your digital devices, or both, do not for one millisecond believe that it is a truthful answer. You ask, "What is your name?" and you hear a sweet little girl's voice say, "Molly." This may or may not answer some of the clients' reports, and it might not be accurate information. What or who you are

speaking with may or may not be named Molly, and might or might not be a little girl. Living people lie, do not expect anything different from those that are in a different condition.

7. When you are in any space that has an audio device actively recording, use your head before you open your mouth. Do not say anything that might come back to haunt you in a much different sense. Remember, other people may be listening to your conversation later, so do not say anything negative about the location, the client, other team members, or say anything too personal that you might not want the public to hear. Also, do not discuss any weaknesses that you have, because the possibility exists that the one nasty little entity that overhears you might use that against you at some point. The bottom line is, think before you speak.

8. Always be polite, and thank them for their time. Courtesy will pay off, and provide extra karma and charisma points.

(A note about provoking for a response: It is simply rude, so I do not recommend that you do it. If there is an entity there that does not want to communicate with you, you should respect that. You are a guest, so you should act like one.)

Photography: Whether you take pictures during the investigation or just before you turn out the lights, photos can be a great tool to document your location and your investigation. It is common practice to take several photos of every part of the location, including the base station. When you take your photos, follow these tips:

1. Always clean your camera lenses before you start taking pictures. There is nothing worse than having to throw away data because of a dirty lens. This also ensures that you do not complete your photo session with the lens cap on.

2. When in a room, stand in the center and take a picture of each wall, the floor, and the ceiling. Imagine that you are trying to create a 3D image of that room.

3. Always take two or more consecutive pictures from the same position. This will ensure that the mist, apparition, shadow figure, orb, or whatever you caught was in the room with you, and not just some dust, smudge, or light beam bouncing off your camera lens.

4. When you are walking around the location taking photos, bring a digital recorder with you. You never know what you might catch in audio, or when you might catch it. It pays to be an opportunist in this field.

5. If you have a lens cap that dangles, try to secure it somehow so it does not make noise when it hits the strap or other objects.

Handheld Video: This includes thermal imaging devices recorded on video. The handheld video with super night shot capability or full-spectrum is one of the best ghost-hunting tools in my opinion. These devices have come a long way over the years, and have really had one of the most major impacts on paranormal investigations. When using handhelds, keep these tips and considerations in mind:

1. Handheld video cameras have audio capabilities, too. Follow the same procedures as you would for conducting an EVP session.

2. Use the camera to cover each space entirely. Pan your camera slowly around each room as you enter them. If possible, try to cover each wall, floor, and ceiling. After full video coverage of the space is complete, you can then focus on a particular area of interest.

3. Do not be quick to videotape yourself or your investigative partner's reactions to stimulus. You are not filming a TV show, so filming the surprised look on your face is not as important as filming what might have caused it.

4. Do not be focused on one interesting object for too long. It is video, not a photograph.

5. With night vision-enabled cameras team members walk about in the dark and see much more clearly than with the naked eye, but the field of vision is reduced, so use caution if this is how you move around. Sure, it will allow you to see that fragile statue dead ahead of you so you do not bump into it, but that gaping hole in the floor is off the view screen. Your video might provide conclusive evidence of the theory of gravity, but that type of evidence would not be groundbreaking.

Instrument Readings: These devices include all EMF meters, temperature and atmospheric testing devices, motion detectors, or any other gadget that you brought with you. In all cases, the readings that you receive should be recorded or logged somehow using your audio recorder, digital camera, DVR system, or a note pad that you carried with you when you took the reading (a bit cumbersome way of doing it). I highly suggest communicating with the base station so it can be recorded in the base log. When you make your reports you should:

1. Report the name of the device (it is vital to know what piece of equipment you are using). If you have more than one device of the same kind, label them so you will know which one was used. One might be more accurate or sensitive than another. Moreover, if you are carrying more than one similar device, report both readings.

2. Report the selected setting. Many devices have more than one setting, and it is imperative to know the selected setting. You need to know which setting to use and what the each of settings measure. You need to know how to use your equipment, even in the dark.

3. Report the reading you received and the unit of measurement. Reporting a reading of 29 is meaningless if you do not know the unit of measurement. Reporting a reading of 29 mG is meaningful and specific.

4. Be very specific when reporting the area that you obtained a reading in. Knowing that you received this reading in the dining room is good. Knowing that you received this reading from the chair at the head of the table in the dining room is better.

5. Report any anomalies that you encountered. That one odd reading might be significant. Your device suddenly stopped working for a reason. The device itself might be faulty, or you might have experienced something significant. At any rate, it needs to be logged into the base log or announced for the benefit of the audio recorder in the space.

An instrument report should appear in the log similar to this example: "2137 Mark reported the single-axis EMF reading of 29 mG in the dining room from the chair at the head of the table. All other readings in that room are 0. Ambient temperature in the room is 67.3°F by probe and 65.2°F at the table." This entry specifies the time of the reading, who took the reading using what device, what the reading was, the units of measurement, and the specific areas measured. When making such log entries, abbreviate as you can, but make sure that your abbreviations can be understood by everyone reading the log later on.

Anecdotal Reports: During your investigation, things may occur that your devices are not designed to pick up. While investigating, your investigative teams might feel dizzy in some areas, uncomfortable, or feel like they are being watched, touched, grabbed, or pulled. These feelings may not be supported by any of your high-tech instrumentation, but are very valid and should be documented. Whether the investigators call in their feelings or sensations to the base station or simply announce them to the audio or video devices in that space, those feelings need to be documented. Personal sensations are a big part of paranormal investigating. In most cases, it was a personal experience that caused you to be involved with the location in the first place. When documenting a personal experience, you should:

1. Note who experienced the event. Some investigators are more sensitive than others; they notice things that others do not. That creepy feeling that they have may be significant even if their investigative partner does not feel the same. Then again, some people have a tendency to let their imaginations run wild, and might experience physiological responses to an internal event occurring within their own psyche. In any case, it is important to document the event and who experienced it. You might not find evidence of paranormal activity, but you might have a case study into the perceived reality that a creepy area can produce in certain suggestible people. That is good data too!

2. Note the time and location the event was experienced. You never know; it might have a direct correlation to some other piece of evidence.

3. Note the specifics of the experience. Sometimes emotional feelings can be hard to articulate, but you have to be able to accurately describe what is

going on. Physical sensations, feeling cold, feeling grabbed, pushed, or touched are a bit easier to describe.

During an investigation with a former team, one of our guest investigators announced to the digital recorders that he felt like he just had his head touched. When the review of the audio was conducted, you could clearly hear what sounded like young female voices saying, "Boo, boo, boo!" and immediately following those voices the investigator said, "I'm pretty sure that I just had my head touched." That situation presents a good example of why it is important to report personal experiences!

Communications: Clear communications are vital to maintain throughout the investigation. Not only are teams communicating with the base station, but also on larger locations, teams need to be able to communicate with other teams. When a team is conducting and EVP session and they hear a thump or a yell from another floor, they need to know if that was a response or something caused by another team investigating a different area of the location. Communications need to be clear, concise, and meaningful. They can get out of hand if people are talking back and forth more than simply investigating, so you need to monitor your radio communications, and take immediate corrective action if they are misused.

A good set of walkie-talkies is an investment in the integrity and safety of your investigation. Not only is this equipment used for reporting data to the base station, it might provide the first notification that someone needs help. Remember, the locations that you investigate are not always safe and not always as abandoned as you think they are. Running into an unexpected person during an investigation in an abandoned building can present just as much of a safety and security concern as finding a rattlesnake in the basement. These are all good reasons for doing a walkthrough of the location when everything is clearly visible beforehand, and maintaining good communications during your investigation.

Various Other Encounters: A team investigating might encounter a number of things. Be prepared to analyze them on the spot if possible. When you encounter something, verbalize it for the benefit of the audio devices you have with you, or for the benefit of the recording devices that are stationary. When you do receive an unexpected event, do not jump to the conclusion that it is paranormal. As you encounter each event, ask yourself some questions and examine all possibilities. If you receive or you encounter:

A cold spot: Try to measure the temperature with a probe thermometer. What is the temperature difference of that spot with the rest of the room? Keep in mind that every room has different heat characteristics. Items in the room, furniture, carpeting, wall composition, etc., all retain heat differently. A reading in the middle of a room a using your probe thermometer may read

65°F but a simultaneous reading on the sofa next to a wall might read 62°F. This does not indicate anything paranormal it merely demonstrates that cold spots exist naturally.

An EMF spike: Using an EMF meter, what is the reading? Is that reading specific to a particular area? Could something be trying to communicate or did some electronic equipment nearby cause the reading?

An apparition, mist, or shadow figure: Ideally, you would want to capture this on video. Though this may be the Holy Grail of any investigation, it can be challenging to deal with at the time without causing urine stains for some. Try to communicate, or if you have lost your nerve, request another team member to deal with it. Someone fearless would be a good choice.

A disembodied voice: Answer it. If it is threatening, try reasoning with it. Threatening or not, hopefully you have it recorded. One thing to keep in mind is that sound travels differently in different locations and conditions. Could that voice been from outside? Could it have been a member of the investigative party?

Glowing orbs, or flashing lights: An interesting phenomenon discussed in the next chapter. Capture it on video if possible, and try to communicate with it even if it is just a dust particle (you really do not have anything to lose, that is why you are there). Ask yourself what was the condition of the room when the lights were on; was it dusty?

Knocking sounds or footsteps: Record them. Announce what you heard. This might be an attempt at communication, or it might be nothing more than the house settling.

Other crazy stuff: This is a realm of infinite possibilities, and it would be impossible to list everything that you might run into. You could run into an infestation of insects, spiders, or rodents; a natural gas leak, leaking pipes, or any number of things that could naturally explain the reported activity. Of course, the previous examples are not as exciting as finding Cthulhu lurking about playing hide-and-go-seek in the basement.

Securing from the Investigation

How you secure and break down from an investigation is just as important as your set up. Accounting for all of the equipment and proper stowage of each piece is vital. Refer to your base station log and your inventory sheet to ensure that everything is accounted for. Load your equipment in your vehicle securely, and make sure that you take everything that you brought with you, including any trash that you might have produced during the time spent at the location.

Before you leave the location, talk with the owner and give him/her a brief of the investigation. You might want to include an estimate of how much data you will have to screen through as well as an idea of when you might be able to discuss any findings (or lack of findings). At this time you might have some suggestions of what the owner may want to do as far as documenting any further occurrences, or if you noted significant problems during the investigation that might warrant inspection or repair.

7 DATA REVIEW

If you asked for a show of hands from your team, or perspective team members to see who would want to go out on an investigation, you would probably see many hands go up. If you asked, who would like to go through all of the data collected, more likely than not, you would not see the same number of hands. Data review is the most tedious part of the process, and sadly, some people avoid it like the plague. Though it can seem as exciting as watching paint dry, it is just as important as conducting the investigation itself.

In most of this book, you find the word 'data' instead of the word 'evidence' for a reason. The general definition of the word 'evidence', pertinent to paranormal investigative purposes, is that which tends to prove or disprove something. All too often 'data' is presented or called 'evidence' before it has been critically scrutinized. When you have several hours of video, audio, and photographs to go through from an investigation, it is just 'data.' The only thing you have before you start going through all of that data is circumstantial evidence that you did in fact conduct an investigation, and recorded a lot of audio and video. So let us just call it 'data' for now. This may seem like a very small point, but in my opinion, it is an important one. I would hardly call a cat's litter box with a small lost diamond in it a 'treasure.' However, I guarantee that I would screen through all of that crap carefully to find that one diamond!

Do not ever feel that one person should take on all of the data review. Too often, there is much more than one person can handle in a reasonable amount of time. When it comes to reviewing the data, it is best to divide it up with a few members looking at different pieces at a time. One person might have a real strength with photography, and another might have more of a background in audio. Although it would be wonderful if everyone had

43

strengths in all areas, it just would not be realistic. Some people are simply more observant when it comes to audio, while others have real keen visual observation skills. Like everything else in an investigation, you must really know your team's strengths (and weaknesses) well. Assigning the right person for each job is essential for a successful data review. In addition, that and possessing some real organizational skills is important.

One way to keep things organized is to use some sort of form to keep track of each reviewed file. Such a form is included in the "Useful Forms" chapter. This form identifies the date, investigation location, area that the data was obtained, and the filename of the data. The user simply fills in the form, and includes the time that the video or audio recording was started. From there, the user just needs to start reviewing the file, and notes when and what was discovered. The file type would dictate what you are to do with that piece of data. There is nothing magical about the form itself; you could just as easily use a piece of scratch paper, a napkin, or on the blank pages of this book. The "Data Review Sheet" form, as well as all of the other forms supplied with this book, is simply a tool to help you develop your own methods. No doubt, you may develop forms and tools of your own that suit your particular needs better!

Here is an example of a Data Review Sheet showing how helpful it is to maintain information integrity and keep your data organized:

Data Review Sheet

Date: 2 Feb 2012			Location: Townsend Hotel - Rm 301	
Data type:	X	Audio		Video
		DVR		Camcorder no.
Device source:	X	Digital recorder no. 4		
1848:30	← Time recording started		Filename:20120202-301.mp3	
Time of Event	(Description of Event, Duration, Other Data)			
+1:28:26	Voice! Male voice says "I hear you." Intelligent response? File: 301-2016.56.mp3			
+2:02:01	Knock. Shave and a haircut response. File: 301-2050.31.mp3			
+3:05:56	End of file.			

In the example above, the Data Review Sheet notes the date and the location of the obtained data. It also notes that it was an audio file from digital recorder number 4. The recording started at 1848 and 30 seconds (6:48 PM). As the reviewer was listening to the file, the first oddity was noted 1 hour 28 minutes and 26 seconds into the recording, a male voice saying, "I hear you." The reviewer created a new file so that snippet of audio could be played at a team review. The reviewer labeled the new file with the location (room 301), and then added the time that data was located on the recording to the start time to arrive at the actual time (2016:56 or 8:16PM and 56 seconds). Not everyone uses military time for their files, but it does help for long investigations that go past midnight. The second piece of data was heard 2 hours and 2 minutes into the original recording. It was a response to the old "shave and a haircut" routine. Once again, the reviewer created a new file for just that segment of audio, and labeled it in the same manner as he did the first one.

(Note: Having the smaller audio files separated allows for a team review of those files. Sometimes the strange voice that you pick up during your review turns out to be that of one of your team members. Everyone on the team should have an opportunity to listen and evaluate what you have found. It might indeed be EVIDENCE of something! Holding a team evidence review before disclosing information with the client is crucial.)

As you and your chosen reviewers go through your data, you catalog all of your files using a similar procedure as described above. You review your DVR system files as well as the handheld camera files logging any oddities. Once you have completed your review, opened the new files up for scrutiny by your team members, you might then have evidence that will help answer the client's questions (or perhaps raise some new ones).

Review Tips

Whether you are reviewing audio or video data (including thermal), you need to have a few things available to you for a good review. You need a comfortable workspace; you are going to be there for a while so you should be comfortable. Your review area should be quiet and free from distractions. The space should be well lit, but not cause any glare or discomfort on your monitor(s). Have some water and some snacks ready. You need to make sure that you have had plenty of sleep and are alert. Reviewing all the data that you have collected during your investigation is going to take a lot of concentration, patience, and time. Stay fresh by taking breaks, stand up and walk around, do some push-ups, or whatever else will keep your blood flowing. Going through all of this data is like a treasure hunt; you have to dig for a long time to find that one gold nugget! Along the way, you will probably find some pyrite, too. With experience, you will know the difference.

Audio Review. Reviewing audio requires time, concentration, and patience. Conducting a good audio review also requires some software. Certainly, you could just plug in a set of headphones into your digital recorder and listen to it that way, but how are you going to share that one gem of audio where a disembodied voice is telling you to get out? If you simply tell someone about it, it is not evidence; it is hearsay or just another ghost story. You need to be able to share the file somehow.

Using software designed for audio editing allows you to copy the segments that you find in your original file, and create a new one that has your audio of interest isolated from the rest of the file. Most digital recorders have a USB connection. Simply follow the manufacturer's directions, and download your audio files to your computer. There are several inexpensive programs that you can obtain from the Internet to use for your review. Find one that will allow you to export files in mp3 format in CD quality, be able to display the waveform of the audio file, and provide a method of increasing the volume of specific areas within the file. You do not need to be a sound engineer to operate this software; it just takes a little practice to be a competent user.

When you have your file opened up in your audio editing software, set it to waveform view. This allows you to see what is going on with the audio. Eventually, you will begin to see sounds in the file before you hear them. You might see long stretches of a flat line, then a couple of spikes. Those spikes mean that there is a sound there, so simply highlight that area and listen to it; it might be something, then again perhaps not. In all cases though, there is something there and whether it is a voice, knock, wind, moan, or the joints of older investigators popping, you need to be able to identify it.

Let us say you are reviewing your audio, and you come across a voice that does not sound like anyone on your team in an area verified as unoccupied. You take a quick glance at the base station log (see why this is important?) and notice that no team members were in that area. You feel that you have something good, so you fill out your data review sheet entries and make a new file. Later, you play that file for your team, and everyone agrees that it is not any team member's voice and everyone agrees on what was said in that file (which is rare). Now that your team agrees, you should have a method of annotating the file's quality. Such a class method, originated by Sarah Estep in 1982, exists:

Class A = Clearly understood, little to no modification necessary.

Class B = Good quality, but requires minor modification (volume or noise reduction)

Class C = Poor quality, requires significant modification (could be something else)

It is an odd circumstance that a Class C piece of audio evidence would be shown to the client, unless of course that is all you received the entire night. It happens unfortunately.

(Note: Avoid eating while conducting an audio review. If you cannot help yourself, then avoid crunchy foods, even if you are as addicted to eating wasabi peas as much as I am. Not only do those crunchy little morsels of deliciousness interfere with hearing faint sounds making you miss something important, some of them are so hard that they can break a tooth! Imagine my dumb explanation to my dentist...)

Video Review: For some reason, video review seems a bit more fun. It still takes the same amount, more perhaps, of concentration as audio does, but the time seems to move a little faster (to me). Whether you are looking at video data from your DVR system or handheld cameras, the review procedure using a data review sheet is the same. If your video footage has audio, you are listening at the same time. I have received audio data from my video camera that was later introduced to my team as EVP evidence! There is a lot going on when you review video, and that is probably why I think it is more fun to review.

If you had a well-manned base station during your investigation, the log keeping maintained, and someone was really paying attention to the DVR display, your DVR review will be more precise. With an accurate base log, you will know the times to pay attention to particular events. When you review video footage (DVR or handheld), you are looking for visual changes in the field of view. These changes can be objects moving inexplicably, shadows that become visible though there was no change in the light source, mists that appear, move, or disappear without an apparent cause, or any other unexplainable visual phenomenon. Common anomalies found in almost every investigation are these spherical objects called orbs. Orbs are one of the most controversial phenomena that virtually everyone captures, so I think they deserve some discussion.

Orbs can appear in photographs or video. They are usually characterized as circular objects that appear singularly or in great numbers, and have some movement to them. More often than not, these orbs are merely dust particles or water vapor droplets that are very close to the camera lens. In dusty locations, you will see millions of small dust particles that are reflecting the IR light from your camera. In some ways, this is very helpful to see the airflow in a particular space, which might explain other reports of activity. On very rare occasions though, orbs do things that capture your attention.

There are many investigative teams that study the orb phenomenon, and rightly so! Imagine that you are watching your DVR monitor display the camera view from a dark basement. That sea of dust particles reflecting IR light that float from the right side of the screen to the left during video review establishes airflow. Suddenly, from the top of the screen there is a larger orb that seems to give off its own light, and heads directly away from the camera and into the next room contrary to the established airflow. Is that dust or water vapor? Personally, I do not think so. It could be a flying insect or something else entirely.

On a previous investigation, we recorded some orbs; some of them blinking that followed a purposeful path in a deserted space and against the predominant airflow. Later in that investigation, one investigator who was conducting an EVP session in front of one of our DVR cameras had a physical response to an orb. Watching the DVR footage, the orb started out on the left side of the screen and very slowly floated his direction. When the orb reached his body, he lurched forward a bit, and reported that he felt like he had been hit in the back. On another investigation, we have recorded orbs perform some aerodynamic acrobatics that simply did not make sense with regard to the air flow, and even observed one orb change direction and seemed to inspect some toys we had placed in a room as trigger objects. Orbs may be significant, so if you capture some on video that might explain something, you might be able to present it as evidence (though I am unsure of what it is evidence of). It would certainly be a stronger piece of evidence if you captured an EVP or EMF spike at the same time.

If you have a compelling piece of video from a DVR system, more often than not, it will not have audio attached to it. This is why you place a digital recorder with you DVR cameras, and announce the DVR time when you start recording on your device. Tying the video and audio together creates a much more powerful piece of evidence than the video or audio alone. I suggest that you find some software that will enable you to mate audio and video together in order to powerfully share your evidence. There are many software titles available for video editing, and most of them are capable of mating your video and audio as a single file. I make no recommendations for any software in particular, do your research and find one that is simple to use. I feel that the software that is labeled "FREE" is probably good enough to get the job done.

Base Log Review: When you are taking EMF, temperature, and other readings, it is important that these readings are logged somewhere. I highly suggest putting them in your base log so that you do not have more logs to file later on. Going through this log might help explain some of the reported activity, or provide some amplifying data to your audio or visual evidence. The information from your instruments may be used in your debrief with your client, and might explain some things that were not initially reported to you.

High EMF fields have been reportedly associated with several health issues. Exposure to areas with high EMF is believed to cause feelings of anxiety, nausea, and general uneasiness; the report of feeling 'creeped out' is common. Our team investigated a location where the report of hair standing up on the back of the neck and the feeling of being followed was reported by more than one occupant. When we investigated, we found that the new commercial carpet was laid without padding on an old wooden floor. When you walked on that carpeting, there was so much static electricity created that the hairs on the back of your arms and neck stood up. When a person walked on the floor, the wood was compressed. A step or two later, and that compressed wood popped back into place. It presented a creepy feeling of being followed, and the standing hairs seemingly suggested that the event was paranormal. It wasn't.

After you have all of your video, audio, and instrument review completed, it is a good idea to compare your Data Review Sheets to your base log. You might find some surprising correlations that will strengthen or weaken what you might consider evidence. Your "Class A" EVP that you found in your review will be a stronger piece of evidence if you are positive that the voice was not one of your team members. Hopefully, your base log was solid enough to support knowing where all of your team was at all times. With regard to evidential data, if in doubt, throw it out. Do not compromise the integrity of your investigation and your team's name with shoddy evidence.

Team Review: The evidence that you will present to your client, proudly post to your website, and share with other paranormal investigative teams needs to stand up to critical review. You and your team are the first line of critics, and you must be able to support your findings. In a sense, you need to be your biggest critic. Admittedly, this is tough to do, especially when you are new to this field! When you get that first clear EVP, you are going to be ecstatic! That first video clip of a shadow figure is going to make you do a back flip! That clear image of an apparition in period clothing is going to shoot butterflies out your bottom! However, despite all of that wonderful excitement, you have to remain calm, look at it with neutrality and attempt to debunk it every step of the way. Trust me: everyone that you share that evidence with will be looking for an alternative explanation, so try to beat them to the punch. If you cannot find remotely possible alternatives that would explain the evidence, then you may have something valuable there!

The best critical tool that you have is the Team Review. Get together with the team and share your information. Critically discuss and debate your evidence video clip by video clip, audio bite by audio bite, and whatever other data you consider evidence. This can be as tedious as the initial review, but now you are bringing in everyone to the process, and you have a lot less data to deal with. As you play each audio clip, ask if everyone agrees with what it says. Did everyone see the same thing in the video clip? What could each of these things mean? During this review with your team, you might be upgrading or downgrading the class of your EVPs, and assigning meaning to what you have seen or heard. Everyone approaches evidence from a different perspective. Take advantage of that when you have your team together.

When you and your team have reviewed all that you found, it is time to start thinking about what to do with it. Each piece of evidence that you identified and commented on should have some meaning; it should be evidence of something. As a group, you need to decide what all this evidence proves. A final question to ask your team, "Did we accomplish our investigative goal?" I hope that you can honestly answer 'yes.'

Now that you have gone through all of your data and isolated the audio, video, instrumental, and anecdotal evidence, and you and your team have reviewed all of that evidence and reassigned meaning to each of them, your next step is to figure out how to present that evidence to your client and/or present it to the public. Whether you call this presentation a "reveal," a "debrief," an "investigation report," or anything else, this is the bow that ties this investigative package together.

8 THE INVESTIGATION REPORT

The report of your investigation needs to be professional and thorough. This report to any reader must clearly explain what was going on at the location that caused you to be called in, who was called in to examine the situation, what was done, what was found, and when it happened. This report is where all of the pieces of the investigation come together to provide evidence that Colonel Mustard did it in the Conservatory with the candlestick! There are many ways to write such a report and present your evidence to the client and the public. Some teams display their result on their team's webpage, while others strictly on YouTube. In either case, you need to be able to sit down with your client and present your findings before you broadcast it everywhere.

It would be a good idea if you had a set template for writing your report. That way you could just plug in your data for each investigation and print it out. It is also customary to provide the client with a copy of your evidence once you have displayed it. No doubt, your client will be as excited as you are to share this information with family and friends. Providing a hardcopy report of the investigation and a DVD of the audio and video evidence that you have collected is a great way to present the data. This souvenir-type debrief will make you popular if you have the capability of creating one. Nevertheless, whether you present the evidence on DVD or just a CD of the audio and video files, you need to have a written report to account for the investigation.

It is important that your report accurately reflect the events and conditions that you and your team experienced. Your report should include:

1. *The date, time, and location of the investigation.* The client might not want this disclosed for public viewing. If you publish your report on your website for everyone to read, you need to be clear with your client that you are going to do this. Some homeowners and business owners might not want people to know that there was a paranormal investigation conducted at their home or

business. It could be damaging to their reputation, the possible sale of their property, or result in financial loss. Be respectful of this and do not publish specifics or information that would allude to a specific property or business. Stating that the investigation was at a bakery in a small town that has only one bakery would be as specific as noting the name and address of the bakery. In such a case, just note it was a private business in whatever county. Alternatively, if it was a home, list it as a private residence in whatever city. This maintains their privacy and keeps the paranormal vulture teams away (and there are a few always circling about looking for scraps). If you have permission to disclose the location and that permission is in writing, then do so.

2. *The team members conducting the investigation.* It is important to note this. People want to know who was in their home, business, or on their property. Also, team members like to keep track of the investigations that they have been involved in.

3. *The weather and any possibly significant astronomical event.* It has been said that paranormal activity has increased during particular weather events like thunderstorms, during different phases of the moon, and during/after major solar events. I personally do not know if that is true or not, but the only way to tell is to add to the data and see if there is some sort of correlation. This is your big chance to participate in such a data gathering exercise.

4. *A general description of the reported activity.* You do not need to be too specific here. The client already knows what was reported. Your generalizations here are more for the benefit of others reading your report.

5. *The investigative goal.* The investigative goal explains why you are there and determines whether your investigation was successful or not.

6. *A chronological brief of the investigation.* This is simply a brief summary that highlights the important aspects of the investigation. Though attention to detail is of the most importance for team records, the property owner does not need to be burdened with all of the details.

7. *A summary of the anecdotal, instrumentation, audio and video evidence.* This section gives you the opportunity to be specific with your findings. Evidence received simultaneously on different media is especially important to note here. Instead of just filling this section with all of your readings, keep it to what is important with regard to the investigation.

8. *Any conclusions that you might have arrived at.* The conclusion of your investigation with regard to the reported activity and the evidence that you collected should address the points of your investigative goal.

In chapter 6, you were introduced to the Andbeanie family and the activity that the family was experiencing. Using the data in the Example Questionnaire and Investigation Plan, the team created a plan and conducted an investigation. The following example Investigation Report was delivered to the client:

Investigation Report

<u>Date</u>: 10 March 2011
<u>Time</u>: 7:13-11:39PM
<u>Location</u>: Private residence, Anytown, WA
<u>Investigative Team</u>: Michael, Kathy, Mark, Alex, & Ann
<u>Weather and Astronomical Data</u>: Partly cloudy skies, temperature ranging from 46F to 40F. Lunar phase: Crescent waxing. No solar activity noted.

<u>Reported Activity</u>: The occupants hear whispering in the kitchen mostly at night, there are feelings of being watched while at the dinner table, and there are reports of physical contact in the kitchen and hallway of a non-aggressive nature.

<u>Investigation Goal</u>: The investigation was conducted to document the whispering in the kitchen, the unusual emotional feelings in the dining room, and to discover what might be causing these sounds, feelings, and physical sensations.

<u>Investigation Events</u>: The team arrived at 7:13 PM and met with the owner. After a tour of the location, the investigation base station was set up in the garage. Four IR DVR cameras were set up in the kitchen, dining room, hallway, and living room. A digital audio recorder was placed near each DVR camera. The investigative teams went out in pairs with only one team inside the residence at any given time. EMF readings and photographs were taken before and during the investigation. Investigative teams rotated in and out of the residence approximately each half hour. The investigation was concluded at 11:39 PM."

<u>Investigation Summary</u>: Throughout the investigation, each team that sat at the dining table reported feeling "a bit off" or "creeped out." EMF readings on the ceiling fan were 5 mG with the lights and fan off, 12 mG with the lights on and the fan off, and 68 mG with the lights and fan on in low speed. All EMF readings were 0 when the breaker to that room was shut off during the investigation.

While in the hallway, Kathy reported hearing whispering in the kitchen. Review of the dining room audio confirmed the sounds of whispering at the same time. The audio recorder in the kitchen showed that it was mechanical in nature and would occur every 35 minutes.

Alex reported feeling like his arm hair was being touched in the hallway. Using a piece of tissue in the hallway, a strong air current running approximately 3 ½ feet above the floor was discovered, caused by the forced air heating system in the upper wall of the hallway.

A Class B EVP was obtained at 10:12PM in the living room of a woman's voice saying: "Come here."

Conclusions: After the investigation, the reported activity was found to have natural origins. The sounds of whispering in the kitchen were decidedly caused by the compressor in the refrigerator, as these sounds were picked up in the kitchen as the compressor cycled. From a distance, the refrigerator cycling to maintain temperature sounded much like whispering, and it was understandable that the client thought that it was paranormal in origin.

The feelings of being watched and uneasiness in the dining room was reported by the client and felt by the investigative team members. The unusually high EMF readings coming from the ceiling fan could easily cause these feelings. The ceiling fan motor and the CFL bulbs in the light housing of the fan read a maximum of 68 mG. When the breaker to the dining room was off, investigators at the table did not feel any emotional effect. Recommend having an electrician inspect the wiring to the ceiling fan.

The one EVP received did not necessarily explain any of the reported activity, and it occurred at a point in the investigation when no one was in the home. Though faint, the voice was clear from the recorder in the living room and was not on any other device. It is possible that the voice came from outside the home. Recommend observation outside the home between the hours of 10PM and 11PM to see if someone routinely walks his or her dog at that time because the voice sounded more like a command than a conversational tone.

Conducting a Reveal

Whether you call this a reveal, debrief, or anything else, this final meeting with the client brings closure to your investigative event. This meeting involves one or two team representatives, the client that called you in to investigate, and/or the owner of a location. This is a very easy meeting to conduct, because if you have a thorough investigative report written, you only need to read it. Additionally, you may want to present audio and/or video that you have considered evidence of paranormal activity. When you have completed your presentation, answered any additional questions that the client may have, you conclude your meeting by giving your client three important items:

1. *A copy of the Investigation Report.*

2. *A copy of your audio and/or video evidence on CD or DVD* (limited to what seems appropriate as evidence supporting the investigative goal).

3. *A Public Release of Information form.* Some teams have the client sign this before the investigation starts. Personally, I think that is in the best interests of the client to sign this form after they have viewed the evidence. This allows the client to determine what can be released to the public and what cannot. Obtaining data during an investigation is what you are there for. Once the data is scrutinized and you have what you consider evidence of something, you will want to share it. You need to be clear with the owner on what you can share and what you cannot. You might be able to share audio EVP files or video captures, but not the location of where you obtained them, which is particularly true in private residences and businesses. Keep in mind that not everyone finds paranormal evidence intriguing; some people react to it very negatively. Publishing your findings with the name of the client, the address of the location, or the name of the business may cause the client problems in their personal and/or professional life. Be clear with the client, and just as you look out for the best interests of your team, keep the client's best interests in mind also.

Evidence/Media Presentation

When creating a DVD or CD of the evidence for the client, or posting your evidence on the Internet via YouTube or other media outlet, try to refrain from being dramatic. If you search the internet for paranormal investigation videos, you will find quite a few, and several of them are nothing more than low budget ghost flicks. If you want to be taken seriously throughout the paranormal community and desire to contribute to the paranormal investigative field, please take these recommendations when creating media for public display:

1. Present your data without trying to emotionally manipulate the viewer. This includes using creepy fonts, presenting narrative designed to influence, and adding musical soundtracks. When you are trying to connect a scary feel to the evidence you are sharing, you have crossed the line from investigator to entertainer. No longer are you a legitimate investigator of paranormal phenomenon as much as a producer of a low-budget paranormal-related show. Your reputation as an investigator will suffer greatly if you produce such videos, and few people will take your evidence seriously.

2. Let the evidence speak for itself. Do not embellish the data; let the viewers or listeners come up with their own conclusions.

3. Provide the viewer with some contact information at the end of the video so if they have questions or would like to review the raw data they can do so. Chances are that a sound engineer that is a fellow paranormal investigator might have better equipment and software to evaluate that EVP that you are so proud of. Provide them with a copy, and take his or her comments cheerfully. It might become a stronger piece of paranormal

evidence, or it may be downgraded significantly; in any case, a professional looking at your evidence is a great honor!

4. If your findings are of significant, consider submitting them to the Library of Congress.

9 THE PARANORMAL COMMUNITY

I cannot think of a field of interest that does not have its own social community of like-minded people; paranormal investigators are no different. Paranormal investigators come from all walks of life and cover just about every demographic. We range from the very normal to the kind of weird; collectively we might be compared to the Island of Misfit Toys. We represent a small fraction of the population, but there are a lot of us. In fact, we are a thriving community that holds conventions, conferences, and other activities. If you are just getting into the field, I highly recommend that you search for and attend an event in your local area.

Sometimes these events are difficult to find. One of the reasons that these events are difficult to find is that there is no corporate sponsorship for advertising. Without that financial backing, all advertising of such an event must come from the people hosting and attending the event. Since most of us do this as a hobby in our spare time, advertising on television or other costly media outlets are out of our financial reach. To look for an event in or near your location, start with an internet search. If there are free newspapers for your area, you might check those out, too.

In 2012, I attended the annual Oregon Ghost Conference in Oregon City, where I gave a short lecture on psychoacoustics and auditory pareidolia. William Becker and Rocky Smith, who provide ghost tours of that city, hosted the conference. The conference featured guest speakers, writers of fiction, paranormal teams, and various classes for all age groups. This conference also featured ghost tours, and allowed the general public access to teams so they could ask their questions about the paranormal in general. It was a great event!

While I was at this conference, I met some interesting people from different teams. All of these teams had different philosophies and methods for investigating. There were many approaches to the field represented. Some teams had religious overtones, some purely technical, and some presented a fun, thrill-seeking approach to paranormal investigating. Regardless of their philosophical approach, if the investigative methods are sound, I consider their team respectable. Here is a short list of the teams in attendance at the 2012 Oregon Ghost Conference:

Black Wolf Paranormal (www.blackwolf-paranormal.com): Located in Poulsbo, WA, and willing to travel worldwide. "A dedicated team of professionals helping clients by finding answers to their paranormal problems using proven investigative methods."

Bridgetown Paranormal (www.bridgetownparanormal.com): Located in the Portland, OR and Vancouver, WA area serving both Oregon and Washington. "Our goal is to research claims of paranormal activity under the most similar conditions in which they have been reported, from the most objective point of view possible."

International Paranormal Reporting Group (www.iprgc.com): Covers Idaho, Oregon, and Washington. "Educating the community about our scientific methods." - A TAPS family member.

Northwest Ghost Tours (www.nwghosttours.com): Located in Oregon City, OR. "Join us on an investigation of the Oregon Territory's oldest city and first capital as we take you on a journey through some of Downtown Oregon City's most active haunts."

Oregon Ghost Society (OGS) (www.oregonghostsociety.com). "Utilizes the latest in scientific equipment to help our clients prove or disprove evidence of paranormal activity."

Oregon Paranormal (www.oregonparanormal.com): Located in Clackamas County, OR and serving all of Oregon State. "Conscious paranormal investigators looking to educate and support families and individuals who may be experiencing paranormal events."

Paranormal & Occult Research Team (P.O.R.T.) (www.paranormaloccultresearch.com) "P.O.R.T. focuses & helps people in Washington and Oregon. Taking a science-based approach with a healthy dose of skepticism."

South Sound Paranormal Research (SSPR) (www.sspri.org) Steilacoom, Washington. "Helping whoever we can. Paranormal unity."

The Paranormal League of America (www.paranormalleagueofamerica.org): Located in Portland, OR and serving Oregon, Washington, and beyond. "Finest in paranormal repair!"

The P.A.S.T. is Present Paranormal Investigations (www.pastispresent.net): Located in Central WA area and travels for co-investigations to Western Washington and Oregon. "The P.A.S.T. is Present seeks to research the paranormal, assist with paranormal claims and educate clients and the public." The P.A.S.T. is Present is part of the PROS Family and GAC only for communicating with other teams.

Western Oregon Organization of Paranormal Investigators (W.O.O.P.I.) (www.woopi-paranormal-investigators.webs.com) Located and serving the Willamette Valley in Oregon. "Our mission is to investigate and document any evidence of the paranormal while helping to explain what may be happening to those who contact us."

The paranormal community is international. No matter where you call home, you can find a team, a chapter, or a group of individuals that deal with the paranormal in one aspect or another. Remember: the paranormal community is not solely about ghost hunting; everything from UFO enthusiasts to Bigfoot hunters is included. Here are a few links to help you find the community or team near you:

Ghost Stop (www.ghoststop.com): Under "Resources" you may select the tab "Teams in Your Area." Ghost Stop is an online store for paranormal investigative equipment. This store is run by a paranormal investigator for paranormal investigators.

The International Directory of Paranormal Investigators (www.paranormalinvestigators.org): A directory listing of paranormal investigator teams world-wide.

The Paranormal Investigation and Research Group (P.I.R.G.) (sites.google.com/site/paranormalirgsite/contact-info): A directory listing of US paranormal groups as well as many interesting and helpful articles.

Paranormal Societies (www.paranormalsocieties.com): Founded with the intent of creating a comprehensive directory of America's Paranormal Societies. Paranormal Societies are largely non-profit, labor-of-love endeavors, and accordingly, do not have budgets for advertising.

United Paranormal Investigators (UPI-Bringing the Paranormal into the 21st Century) (www. unitedparanormalinternational.ning.com): "A place where all members can come and share, support, and help each other without fear of drama or attack for their beliefs."

Whether you are starting your own team or looking for an established team, you will need to start networking. Getting involved with your local paranormal community is a great way to do that. Sometimes teams will refer clients to other teams because either they have a large caseload, or the client's location is closer to another team. Networking with fellow investigative teams has valuable advantages; it is really a win-win situation. Sometimes a team might have expertise or a piece of equipment that would be pivotal for a particular investigation. Co-investigations with other teams or members of another team are certainly beneficial. Inevitably, at least one of the teams will learn something; whether it is a new approach to investigating, proper use of a piece of equipment, new insight, or philosophy. As I have stated in this handbook, there is no universal way of conducting a paranormal investigation; you can learn something from virtually anyone.

If you have decided that you will look for a group to apply to, go to that team's website (most teams have one), and see if yours and the team's personal philosophies are a good match. Send in a resume of sorts, or follow that team's application procedures. If there is an event nearby, see if you can meet them in person. After speaking with you, if you have read this book, they are going to realize that you are serious, and have a clue concerning what this paranormal investigating gig is all about. I hope that that will work in your favor.

If you have decided to form your own group, welcome to the community! You will find guidance on starting your own group in the next chapter.

10 BUILDING A PARANORMAL TEAM

Paranormal investigating is multi-faceted, and it is unrealistic to believe that one person could be an expert in every aspect of the activity. Some people are qualified to operate and evaluate equipment, and some people are better suited to work with the social aspects of the practice. Some have an interest in historical research, public relations, training, managing, organizing, while others possess strengths in observation. For this reason, people draw their strengths together and form a team.

Much like a business, a paranormal team assigns duties and responsibilities to each team member either formally or informally. Some teams have a team leader, while others simply work together to make all decisions. Some teams are large, and some teams are relatively small. Whether you want to have a large team or a small team depends greatly on you. If you are unsure of the team size that you want, I would suggest that you ask yourself this simple question: Do you prefer going to a large party with many people, or would you prefer spending time with just a few close friends? This may be an oversimplification, but if you know yourself well and you know your comfort level in groups, it might be enough for you to make a decision on the size of the group you establish.

Small Team Considerations: Establishing a small team is a relatively easy task. Since you are dealing with few people, it is much easier to know them well, understand their strengths and weaknesses, and it makes each person vital to the overall success of the team.

Smaller teams spend less time managing people to accomplish tasks, spend less time assessing competencies for each member, and spend less time bouncing schedules back and forth to set up an investigation date. All processes are more streamlined with a smaller group.

Smaller teams also have more effective training programs. It is so much easier teaching one or two people to use audio software to evaluate captured EVPs than it is to teach ten people.

Smaller teams have many advantages over larger teams. Membership agreements can be less formal, dues may not be required, transportation arrangements are simple, and accountability concerns are greatly diminished.

Personality conflicts within smaller groups are rare. People behave differently depending on the number of people in company. When you have a smaller group, the behaviors of the individuals are more likely to be genuine to who they really are.

The disadvantage of having a smaller team boils down to manpower. You just might not have enough people to get the job done sometimes. This is why it is important to network with other teams. If you need more qualified investigators, ask another team if there are a few willing to help. More often than not, there are qualified investigators chomping at the bit for an investigation.

Large Team Considerations: Establishing a large team takes a lot more effort than establishing a smaller team. However, because you have more people and you are able to investigate larger locations, you will find that you spend much of your time directing team efforts rather than investigating. If you enjoy the tactical aspect of directing teams to perform specific tasks more than you enjoy investigating, then perhaps establishing a larger team is right for you.

Large teams are able to collect more data simultaneously. This also means that you will have more data to sift through when the investigative phase is over. If you have an effective training plan and several people to go through the data, then you have a significant advantage over smaller teams.

Training larger numbers of people can be difficult. Training on how to listen to, evaluate, and clip audio files, for instance, requires equipment, time, and software knowledge. If you have a large team and several members that need training, you might be better off conducting more training sessions with a few people at a time. It is also nice if the team members are all familiar with the same equipment and software; this makes discussions and evaluation of evidence easier because everyone would be familiar with the same jargon.

One disadvantage with larger teams is that you might obtain an investigation location that is very small, and only a few people would be able to investigate. This can, and does, cause some disappointment with the members that were not selected to go. Try to develop a system for fairness that will spread the wealth, so to speak.

Another consideration with larger teams investigating a location is cross-contamination. Having so many people in one area makes review of data a bit tricky. Was that knock a response to a question that an investigator asked or was it another investigative team on another floor doing the old "shave and a haircut" routine? Your teams will be filling the audio with their own natural sounds, breathing, walking, talking, etc.

Whether you build a small or large team is entirely a matter of personal choice. If this is the first time you are investigating the paranormal, it might be wiser to join an existing team, but if the only team available to you is not taking new members, or has philosophies that you do not agree with, it may be that you will need to build your own team.

Let us say that you, a budding paranormal adventure seeker, have decided to form a paranormal investigation team for the purpose of researching paranormal activity and documenting that activity objectively. How many members should you have? What does being a member mean? How do you select members? Who does what? Here are some items to have clear thoughts about when establishing your team:

1. A mission statement
2. Team member selection
3. Team member responsibilities
4. Team communications
5. Team meetings
6. Member dues
7. Evidence ownership

Mission Statement

As a founder, if you do not know what your goals are, how can you put together a team of people that share your expectations? This is something YOU need to understand and spell out completely so everyone, you, all members, and the public, understand the purpose of the team. You must have a clear understanding of what your group will do, who will do it, and what to do with all of the evidence you have collected when all is said and done. This is your mission statement. Your mission statement should be short and concise; in just a few sentences, it should be clear to your members and anyone else that reads it.

Example: "The primary mission of XYZ Investigations is to conduct investigations of paranormal activities, provide a paranormal referral service for specialized cases, and provide training to home owners, business owners, and the general public, on how to document and appropriately deal with occurrences of paranormal activity. XYZ does not charge for any services."

In the above example, the reader knows that you conduct paranormal investigations, instruct people on what to do if they have paranormal activity, and provide guidance on dealing with such situations. It also tells the reader that you are willing to do this free of charge. If you do charge for your services, you need to be upfront about it, understand that there are many more teams that do not charge, so be prepared for some experienced competition.

Team Member Selection

Your team members can come from anywhere. They can be family, friends, people you have just met, or someone that answered an ad that you placed. Regardless of where they came from, you need to assess them somehow to see if they are a good fit. When selecting members, do not select like-minded people only; if everyone on the team truly believes every report of paranormal activity is the result of a trapped spirit that is unable to cross over, then your objectivity as a team does not exist. Choosing members with different views entirely, or open to all possibilities, would be a more balanced approach to investigating together. This can be a tricky process as someone that you have just met might not be open to full disclosure of their beliefs or motivations for being on a team.

If you know yourself well, chances are that you are able to read others as well. There are certain chemistries between people that can lead to the success of a group or its downfall. Everyone has positive qualities and negative qualities. Finding and adopting people into your group that have realistic views of themselves will increase your chances of being successful.

Establishing a team, large or small, is a sociological experiment in itself. You are bringing together individuals, each with his or her belief systems and perspectives of the world, and trusting them to represent your team's name, your team's reputation. This is not an easy task, and requires constant vigilance to ensure that everyone is on the same page with regard to purpose, everyone remains professional, and that everyone can positively work harmoniously. Your team may have someone that is a complete skeptic and someone that truly believes in ghosts; you need to make sure that the two can work together to achieve the investigative goal. Team members do not need to be best friends, but they do need to be open-minded, positive, and respect each other's point of view.

When you select a potential candidate to join the team, you should establish some sort of probation period. When someone is new, they really want to show off what he or she are capable of and will put forth a lot of effort to be useful and likable. This might not be a good example of what he or she is really like. You need time to get to know them beyond that first, second, and subsequent impressions. Some teams have six-months probationary periods while others have longer. Whatever length of time you decide to put in place, you need to have a realistic understanding of who that person really is. In addition, even though you may have crowned yourself as the leader wielding supreme executive power, your existing team members should have an equal input into who is accepted as a probationary or full-fledged member.

Member Responsibilities

Each team member should be clear on what his or her responsibilities are on investigations and within the team. These can be typed out as a contract, or in the case of very small teams, verbally communicated. Member responsibilities should be assigned based on the member's abilities; always base the member roles on the person's strengths, and never put someone in a position to fail.

Once the member responsibilities are clearly defined, you should include an ethical code of conduct for all team members to abide by. This code covers many traits and behaviors that are essential to maintain a professional and ethical standard. There are so many traits under this umbrella; honesty, respect, dependability, and trust are just a few. Some teams add this to their member contract. If you do not have member contracts in place, then it should, at a minimum, be a discussion point at one of your first meetings as a team.

Team Communications

Team communications, above all else, must remain honest and open. Members should have the freedom to say anything at meetings without fear of reprisal. Ideally, members would have the tact to bring up sensitive subjects about another member of the team, an investigative method, or a host of other topics, but tact is not always available to the less articulate. An open forum without judgment is always the most productive! Keep in mind though; you might not always hear what you want to hear. Airing out differences of opinions or perceptions, in a non-confrontational setting, even if it is of a very sensitive nature, is the only way to achieve resolution within the team. Maturity of all team members is required to hold things together during stressful times.

Even under the best circumstances, the group might stop functioning well even though you have chosen team members that perform well in meetings and investigations. People change, the group dynamics change, and sometimes people lose their direction. Regardless of the circumstances, when a member starts adversely affecting the team, something must be done about it. You can place a member on probation or terminate the member from the team. Regardless of the method that you chose, the entire team should have some say in the matter. Whenever possible, keep everything "above board" with all members.

Team Meetings

Even though all members of the team may share your passion and enthusiasm, everyone has a personal life. Keep this in mind when scheduling meetings. Holding meetings too often can destroy the zeal for the group and cause some resentment. Not holding meetings often enough can make members lose interest. Twice monthly seems to be a good balance, but if you are investigating together often, you might want to reduce the number of meetings.

Member Dues

You may elect to collect dues for your group. This will help pay for meeting incidentals, equipment, spare copies of *Tobin's Spirit Guide* (did that even get a chuckle?) and whatnot. Collecting dues is your call, but the money you collect needs to be fully accounted for at any time by any contributing member, so keep good records.

Evidence Ownership

Ideally, all evidence gathered from a team investigation belongs to the team, not the individual that happened to obtain the data. If the data was obtained in an investigation where the client has given you and your team permission to conduct an investigation, the rules of evidence ownership can vary. If the client has signed a public release for any evidence that you obtain, then you and your team own the evidence, and you may distribute it responsibly. However, if the client did not sign any release, the client is a co-owner of that evidence, and has equal rights with regard to its distribution.

With all of the above information, you should be able to form a team. Whether you read all of this and create a series of team by-laws and procedures is completely up to you. Please note that the larger your team is, the more work you will have to manage it. At times, it will seem that you are spending more time managing your paranormal group than you are actually going out and investigating. This has led to the downfall of many groups that started out with so much promise.

Just a few things to keep in mind:

Nothing lasts forever. Think about how many friends you have had over your lifetime. People grow and change, and there is nothing wrong with that. People lose focus and interest in things, and sometimes you reach a crossroad with people, and not everyone takes the same path. Though breaking up is hard to do, sometimes it must be done. If your group seems to fall apart, try to do it with dignity and maturity. If possible, leave the bridges standing.

11 USEFUL FORMS

Before I reintroduce these forms, I would like to make a recommendation. I highly recommend that you maintain a binder that has all of your information from each investigation you have conducted. This would include all forms, reports, data (on CD or DVD), and history of the location that you uncovered. Each investigation that you archive should be so thorough that you can recreate every step of the investigation. You should also include every investigation report and printed copies of all of your email correspondence relating to that investigative event. You never know when you will need that information in the future. You might reinvestigate that location, and it would be good to know what you did in the past, what worked, as well as what should be improved. This type of archiving system is relatively easy to set up; you already have everything, and it is just a matter of printing it out. Of course, you could keep all of this information electronically, but paper is not subject to viruses and hard disk crashes. The file format of paper is universal, and paper has its own molecular power supply.

These forms are for your use. You are free to use them as they are, modify them to meet your needs, and you are free to fold, spindle or otherwise mutilate them. The forms are generic enough for you to use them directly from this book if you so desire, but I would recommend transferring them to your computer so you can more easily manipulate and complete them. Of course, this might mean that you would need to go through the tedious process of retyping them, but one good thing about recreating these on your own is that you would be using the word processing program that you normally use and is familiar to you. In the following pages, you will find the forms that should enable you to get your paranormal job done:

Questionnaire and Investigation Plan: This all-encompassing form covers your initial meeting with the client, identifies the type of activity going on, who and what resides at the location, and guides you to prepare your investigation plan. (69-75)

Investigation Permission: This form gives you permission to enter a residence, business, or property for the primary purpose of conducting a paranormal investigation. Did I mention something earlier about having your forms reviewed by a law professional? If I forgot to mention it, this would probably be one of the first forms I would have a law professional review. (76-78)

Base Log: This generic form is used by your base station during your investigations. (79)

Data Review Form. This simple-to-use form allows you to annotate significant events as you review audio and video data. Please know that you are not required to complete an entire sheet for each data file that you review. Instead, simply annotate that you have completed review of one file. Then, log that you have loaded a new filename. I admit, when I review data, I fill this out on my computer as I am reviewing, so I do not print any of these forms until my data review is complete. (80)

Investigation Report Format. This is not a form but a format for reporting your investigation to your client and posting to your personal website. (81)

Public Release of Information. This form, once signed by the owner or duly authorized representative of the owner, authorizes you to publicly display the evidence that you have received during an investigation. This form is normally signed after a reveal has been conducted with the owner, and empowers the property owner with options for release of your evidence. (82)

Questionnaire and Investigation Plan
(All information on this form will be kept confidential)

Client Information

Name of Person Requesting Investigation		Resident of address?		Yes
				No
Phone Number with Area Code		Email Address		

Interview

Case Number:		Date of contact:	
Case Interviewer:		Date of Interview:	
Interview Location:		Interview time:	

Location Information

Street Address			City, State		
Nature of residence:		Home	Does the occupant own or rent the residence?		Own
		Apartment			Rent
		Other (explain):			

Nature of Paranormal Activity (Brief description of what is occurring)

1 of 7

Auditory Events (Explain in details)	Details
Voices	
Calling of a name(s)	
Footsteps	
Strange sounds or growling	
Tapping or knocking	
Conversations with spirit(s)	
Other	
Physical Events (Explain in details)	Details
Being touched, shoved, or grabbed	
Tugging on clothing	
Hair on arms or neck standing on end	
Hot or cold spots	
Objects moving without apparent cause	
Unexplained odors	
Appliances turning on or off	
Doors or windows opening/closing	
Other	

Visual Events (Explain in details)	Details
Apparitions	
Smoky or misty forms	
Shadow figures	
Unexplained lights	
Orbs	
Corner of the eye glimpses	
Other	
Emotional Events (Explain in details)	Details
Intense random thoughts	
Feeling of being watched or followed	
Mood changes (especially in one room)	
Unexplained stress or anxiety	
Unexplained feelings of joy or anger	
Recent anniversary of a significant event	
Other	

2 of 7

Resident Information (List all occupants residing at the residence)

Name	Age			Religion	Yrs lived at address
			Male		
			Female		
Name	Age		Male	Religion	Yrs lived at address
			Female		
Name	Age		Male	Religion	Yrs lived at address
			Female		
Name	Age		Male	Religion	Yrs lived at address
			Female		

(If more entries are needed, use reverse.)

Pet Information (List all pets residing at the residence)

Name	Age			Animal Type	Yrs lived at address
			Male		
			Female		
Name	Age		Male	Animal Type	Yrs lived at address
			Female		
Name	Age		Male	Animal Type	Yrs lived at address
			Female		

Additional Resident Information (Frequent guests, etc.)

3 of 7

Historical Data

Residence and Occupant Background

Date Built (If known)		Previous occupants (If known)			Name(s), contact info, etc.
Is there a history of paranormal activity at the residence?				Yes	If Yes, explain:
				No	
Is there documentation of previous paranormal accounts (newspaper clippings, occupant testimony, etc.)?				Yes	If Yes, explain (attach a copy):
				No	
Any accounts of paranormal activity in the current occupant's previous address?				Yes	If Yes, explain:
				No	
Any known issues with electrical power, heating or cooling systems, or plumbing at the residence?				Yes	If Yes, explain:
				No	
Any known problems with any appliances or electronic equipment at the residence (refrigerator, TV, etc.)?				Yes	If Yes, explain:
				No	
Any history of hoaxing by an occupant or person known to the occupants?				Yes	If Yes, explain:
				No	

Additional Background Information

4 of 7

72

Property Background

Did any significant historic event take place on or near the property?		Yes	If Yes, explain:
		No	
Is there a history of paranormal activity in the vicinity?		Yes	If Yes, explain:
		No	
Is there documentation of previous paranormal accounts (newspaper clippings, etc.)?		Yes	If Yes, explain (attach a copy):
		No	
Does the property reside near a significant man-made structure (high voltage power lines, electrical substation, water pumping station, microwave tower, etc.)?		Yes	If Yes, explain:
		No	
Does the property reside near a major natural feature (creek, river, lake, rock formation, forest, etc.)?		Yes	If Yes, explain:
		No	

Additional Property Information

Investigation Plan

1. Attach a drawing or map of the residence to the back of this form. Mark areas to show known paranormal activity.			
2. What would be the goal of a paranormal investigation?			
3. Are there any off-limit areas in the residence or on the property that you do not want an investigative team to enter?		Yes	If Yes, what area(s):
		No	
4. Do you know of any health or safety issues that might present a danger to an investigative team?		Yes	If Yes, explain:
		No	
5. Are there any special concerns that you have regarding a possible investigation of the residence?		Yes	If Yes, explain:
		No	

Investigation

Date of Scheduled Investigation:		Time of Investigation:	
Assigned Investigators:			

Equipment to Accomplish Goal:

Overall Plan:

Equipment Setup:

EVP Questions:

Investigation Permission

Completion of this form constitutes permission to conduct a paranormal investigation of grounds and structures of the property listed below. All spaces associated with the property are considered open for the purposes of the investigation, unless otherwise noted.

Owner Information

Full Name of Person Granting Permission	Owner or duly authorized representative of the owner?		Yes
			No*
Phone Number with Area Code	Email Address		
* If not the owner or duly authorized representative of the owner, the investigation cannot be conducted until written authorization is obtained by the legal owner, or duly authorized representative of the legal owner.			

Investigation Location

Street Address			City, State		
Nature of residence:		Home	Does the occupant own or rent the residence?		Own
		Apartment			Rent
		Business			Lease
		Other (explain):			
Off-limit areas for investigation:					
Dangerous or hazardous equipment present:					
Safety considerations/concerns:					
Prohibited use items or equipment:					

Investigation Date and Times

Authorized Investigation Date	Authorized Investigation Times

1 of 3

INVESTIGATION AUTHORIZATION

I authorize and grant permission to the below-named investigators to conduct a paranormal investigation of the above property listed as the "Investigation Location" on this document on the date and times listed as the "Investigation Date and Times." The below-named investigators identified as the "Investigation Team" have full use of all facilities, utilities, and equipment on this property with the exception of those listed as "Prohibited use items or equipment." The "Investigation Team" releases the owner or duly authorized representative from liability for injuries and/or damages that might occur during the course of setup, conduct, and securing from the authorized investigative activity.

The investigative personnel listed as the "Investigation Team" assume full responsibility for damages incurred on the property caused by the "Investigation Team" during the course of setup, conduct, and securing from the authorized investigative activity.

The owner or duly authorized representative of the own is responsible for any injury or damage to investigative equipment caused by the owner, duly authorized representative of the owner, employee, or occupant of the property and can be proven responsible for such injury or damage.

Printed name of owner or duly authorized representative (Last, First, Middle):	Signature	Date
Witness (Last, First, Middle):	Signature	Date

CONFIDENTIALITY AGREEMENT

The below-named investigators identified as the "Investigation Team" will protect the confidentiality of all pertinent information, including specific location details, specifics of the paranormal activity, personal information about the client, and any other information that is asked to be kept confidential.

By signing this form we agree to hold all evidence (photographic, video and audio) we capture during this investigation in the strictest of confidence and shall not share said evidence with the public or any other paranormal group unless given permission to do otherwise.

Investigation Team

By signing this document, you agree to the stipulations set forth in the "INVESTIGATION AUTHORIZATION" and "CONFIDENTIALITY AGREEMENT."

Note: If the owner or duly authorized representative of the owner is to accompany the investigative team during setup, conduct, and securing from the investigation, he or she will sign as an investigator, as well as the owner or duly authorized representative of the owner.

Printed name of Investigator (Last, First, Middle Initial):	Signature	Date

Attach additional forms as necessary to accommodate all investigative members.

3 of 3

BASE LOG

Investigation Location		Date:	
		Sheet: of	
Time	Description of Event or Status		

Data Review Sheet

Investigation Date:		Location:	
Data type:	Audio	Video	
	DVR	Camcorder no.	
Device source:	Digital recorder no.		
	← Time recording started	Filename:	
Time of Event	(Description of Event, Duration, Other Data)		

Investigation Report
Format

Investigation Date:

Investigation Times:

Location:

Investigative Team:

Weather and Astronomical Data:

Reported Activity:

Investigation Goal:

Investigation Events:

Investigation Summary:

Conclusions:

Public Release of Information

Client

Full Name of Person Granting Permission	Owner or duly authorized representative of the owner?	Yes
		No
Phone Number with Area Code	Email Address	

Investigation Location

| Street Address | City, State |
| | |

Investigation Date(s):

Paranormal Investigative Team:

As the owner, or duly authorized representative of the owner, listed above as the "Client," I hereby authorize the public release of audio, video, and anecdotal evidence that I have received and/or reviewed, gathered at the "Investigation Location" above, on the "Investigation Date(s)" above, by the "Paranormal Investigative Team" above, under the following conditions:

PUBLIC RELEASE CONDITIONS (Initial those that apply)		
Full release of data: No conditions	Do not publish address of location	
Do not publish owner, occupant or employee names.	Do not publish a specific file(s) (Specify below in Other block)	
Other:		
Printed name of owner or duly authorized representative (Last, First, Middle):	Signature	Date
Witness (Last, First, Middle):	Signature	Date

12 EVP SESSIONS AND SPIRIT BOXES

EVP Session Recommendations

Though I have provided a general description for conducting EVP sessions in chapter six, I would like to propose some considerations and recommendations that will make your session a bit more effective.

1. Never ask leading questions. Even though you have a multitude of information regarding the name of a particular entity that is said to haunt a location, do not use that name when you ask questions. When you supply the answer within a question, an answer that you want to hear to confirm some information that you already know, you will probably get the answer that you wanted. The received answer, regardless of how clearly you recorded it, is essentially meaningless. For example, if you asked a small child, "Are you four?" in order to determine the child's age, you might receive a resounding "Yes, I'm four!" That really does not mean that the child understands the whole concept of age, it simply means that the child answered you with the number that you supplied within your question.

When you ask an open-ended question, and you receive a response that confirms earlier reports, you have a more interesting piece of evidence! To illustrate this statement, let us say that you are investigating a house that has a long history of haunting by a man named Nathaniel. When you are conducting an EVP session, it would be much better if you asked identification questions that were open-ended. "What is your name?" would be a better question than, "Is Nathaniel here?" Receiving an EVP saying "Yes," does not really provide a specific answer to, "Is Nathaniel here?" Receiving an EVP of, "Nathaniel," when you asked for a name, provides specific evidence that confirms earlier reports.

Leading questions are not limited to names but also extend to circumstantial situations. A very common question asked by paranormal investigators during EVP sessions is, "Did you die here?" The implications of this question are almost limitless. This question represents a certain mindset on behalf of the investigator that assumes that the cause of all paranormal activity centers on ghosts or disembodied spirits. This view is very narrow in my opinion; the cause of paranormal activity has infinite possibilities including unconscious manifestations created by the living. In addition to being limited in scope, asking a question regarding the possible entity's demise might be psychologically damaging! What if, for instance, the entity that you are talking to is not aware that it has passed on (if indeed it was once a living being from our realm of understanding)? Asking, "Why are you here?", or "What happened to you?" might yield better responses without involving biased, negative, and possibly traumatic assumptions.

2. Use prepared questions. The first few EVP sessions you conduct are going to be awkward. You are going to feel a bit silly standing around in the dark asking questions to what seems to be no one. Often, you will find yourself in situations that will tax your senses and sensibilities that could cause you to draw a blank. Standing around in the dark staring blankly into the blackness hardly adds to the investigative goal. I cannot stress enough the importance of having some EVP questions prepared before you conduct your sessions. Having a set of questions prepared will save you in such a situation.

3. Use code words. While you are investigating in the dark, you are going to make noises that you did not intend to. You are going to bump into something, knock something over, or your body is going to surprise you with an interesting sound. If you do not announce that you have just entered an accidental noise into your investigation at the time it may be confusing for the person listening to your audio data from that investigation later. Having a code word or two for such an occurrence, something that is understood by the entire investigative party is very helpful. These words should be short and easy to understand. I personally would like to incorporate the word, "Narf!" into my investigations.

4. Use code names. Though it may sound like you are attempting to act like a secret agent or acting out a scene from movie, using code names for your investigative party can be very helpful in several ways. Almost every experienced paranormal investigative team has received EVPs that call out one or more of the investigator's names. The assumption of course is that these disembodied voices are trying to make contact with the named investigator. Personally, I do not like assumptions, because they limit the possibilities. If Bill and Karen are investigating and a voice from the darkness calls out "Bill," chances are that Bill is going to take this personally. The fact that the name Bill is short for William, which is one of the most common names for men, might not occur to Bill and Karen during the investigation. Some of the possibilities in this situation include: The entity that called out the name Bill might have been introducing himself; one spirit might have

been calling another spirit who happened to be named Bill; Bill's father who happens to live a thousand miles away might have psychically projected his thoughts either purposely or subconsciously; a residual feeling from overwhelming debt might have resulted in the word "bill" being used at some point; or a host of other possi-"bill"-ities (I couldn't resist that one).

If you use code names for your investigative team and you receive a voice or EVP calling one of your code names, it takes on a completely new meaning. Code names should be short and uncommon to general conversation. To illustrate this suggestion, Bill and Karen are referred to as "Digit" and "Oyster" throughout an investigation. Later, upon data review, an EVP was recorded that clearly says, "Oyster," and it did not sound like Bill or anyone else in the investigative party. This EVP would indicate that whoever or whatever said that name was intelligent, not residual, and that by virtue of calling a specific name of a person, had intent. You may speculate on the motive or intent as much as you want, but the fact is that someone or something called that obscure word. That alone is significant!

5. Use background noises to your advantage. Though sometimes it may be frustratingly difficult to hear through background noises during an investigation and post review, it can lead you to new discoveries. One of the major reasons that paranormal investigations are conducted at night is that manmade noises and lights are reduced significantly. Though reduced, there are still passing cars and trains, planes and helicopters flying overhead, and people walking and talking on the street. There are also crickets and frogs to contend with. Manmade sounds are a bit more random compared to the natural sounds of crickets and croaking frogs. When investigating and during data review, train yourself to listen between the sounds. If the crickets or frogs are making noises continuously and then suddenly stop, you have an indication that something has changed. Pay particular attention to the silence during these periods, because they just might lead to a significant discovery. Compare the times of the background noise change to other data you might have received. That report of a growling sound or strange vibration felt in the house might have a natural cause.

6. Call for help. Undoubtedly you have watched at least one paranormal investigation reality show where someone heard or received an EVP asking for help. The investigators confirmed that they heard someone ask for help, and then they continued with their investigation. I have a problem with that. If I were driving along and saw an accident take place, I would see if the people involved needed assistance. If they said that they needed help, I know that I would not simply acknowledge that they needed help and then drive away; I would help them as best as I could. The same should go for unseen entities.

The possibility exists that you might not realize that you have received a call for help until you conduct your data review. Without exposing my personal beliefs on the subject, I will just say this: as a spiritual being, you have an obligation to other spiritual beings. If someone or something asks for your help, you should help them or it. The biggest problem with this is that what assistance you can offer is difficult to define. If you cannot define the problem, the solution certainly is not going to come easily; in such a case, you should consult someone that might be able to communicate directly with whomever or whatever is making the plea. With the nature of the problem discovered, you might be able to assist with a solution.

Spirit Boxes

First things first: a "Spirit Box," or sometimes-called "Ghost Box," is not a specialized piece of equipment designed to capture spirit voices. It is simply a radio frequency scanner. The major difference between a device that scans radio signals and a spirit box has everything to do with its price tag and nothing to do with a difference of function. The basic premise behind the device is that it allows spirits to manipulate the white noise in order to communicate. In my opinion, if there was ever a device designed to prove auditory pareidolia, this is it. However, having said that, I must admit that I have heard some interesting responses coming from such a device.

While we were on an investigation, one of my most trusted investigators announced that he felt like someone was touching his head. Within two seconds of making that announcement, the spirit box he was holding clearly blurted out one word, "bald." The fact that he felt as if someone was touching his head combined with the fact that he does indeed shave his head, made that spirit box announcement a compelling piece of data. Did it prove that we were in direct communication with the spirit world? No, it did not. Was it interesting and quite humorous? Yes, we thought it was very interesting, pertinent, and very funny.

I have used this device on investigations, and it has performed as advertised. I have also received just one or two word responses, just a few fragments of words, and on very rare occasions, a full sentence, but most of the time the responses from the device were limited. I can easily understand how some investigators would infer a larger conversational meaning perhaps believing that they were in direct communication with the spirit world, so I understand the device's popularity. Should you use such a device, do not let it become the sole basis for the entire investigation. Try not to impose your own inferences on what you receive. If you received direct answers to direct questions, then you have a more solid piece of data to add to your investigative puzzle.

To add credibility to responses that you receive, I suggest that you take note of the band frequency at the time you receive it. Receiving what seems to be an intelligent announcement to a question, or a pertinent statement while using this device without determining the frequency, makes this a flimsy piece of evidence at best. When you have the frequency and band (AM or FM), you are able to take a standard radio receiver and tune into that station and its neighboring frequencies. More often than not, you will find that what you heard was probably a short snippet of a sentence from a regular broadcast. If you do not find a broadcasting station on or near that frequency, then you might have something, but you would never know for certain unless you check.

From my personal experience with an SB7 device, I can say that I favored the AM setting at 150ms forward sweep rate. AM has fewer stations, and the output voices seems clearer and less cluttered by frequency noise. Your success with this type of equipment will depend on your location, your familiarity with the device, and your susceptibility to auditory pareidolia.

13 PERSONAL EXPERIENCES

Everyone who has conducted a paranormal investigation has experienced something of a personal nature. A personal experience is a feeling, physical sensation, or perhaps a thought, that is limited to just one person. Walking into a dark room and an investigator suddenly feels different; he or she is having a personal experience. Often, investigators will report feeling "off" in certain locations. When someone reports this type of feeling, it generally means that they are experiencing something abnormal but cannot articulate it in the moment. Whenever possible, document personal experiences as they happen as an anecdotal report, as they can be significant later on.

I have my share of personal experiences; one that I would like to share involved handholding. I was with a team conducting an investigation at an old tuberculosis sanatorium. While walking through the location with the current owner, we stopped in what was once a sunroom for female patients. The room faced west and the setting sun provided ample explanation of why this room was warmer than the rest of the establishment. While I was standing there, and as the setting sun was bathing the room in a warm orange cast, I felt a strange, but familiar sensation. As a father, I know what a child's hand feels like when it holds mine, and this was no different. I looked down at my right hand that was loosely at my side, and saw nothing. Yet, I could feel the cool, not cold, delicate fingers within my palm, and a small thumb gently putting pressure on the top of my hand. I could even tell that this was a left hand holding my right. I did neither flinch nor draw attention to myself at all, deciding to savor this one moment that might bring some comfort to a small child. My mind was telling me that this was a little girl.

Our group continued the tour of the location, and I was not paying any attention to our host at all; my mind fixed on the sensations that I was feeling in my right hand. Now and then I would look down, guessing where this little girl's face would be, and I would smile; essentially sharing the moment with her as if it were our private little joke. After several minutes passed, walking around with this little girl as if she was giving me the grand tour, I felt her hand slip out of mine. Whatever she wanted to accomplish was complete, and at that time I shared my experience with the rest of the team.

Even during the event, I fully recognized the implications of the interaction. I know it is very possible that this event was completely my mind playing tricks on me. I have a great and vivid imagination, and this could have been caused by the combination of the location, an accurate account of what my own daughter's hand felt like within mine, and the overwhelming compassion I felt toward the patients of this establishment, especially the children. It could have all been in my head!

If it was indeed in my head, is it possible that those thoughts and feelings were transmitted directly into my mind? The nerves of my right hand, normally sending electrical signals of sensation to my brain (an organ that functions on electrical impulses), could have been bypassed entirely, tricking my brain into the sensation of handholding. My mind may have filled in the blanks with the cause (meaning the little girl's hand), because that was a known sensation, a powerfully tender memory that might have made the whole event seem so real (a downfall of being able to have lucid dreams is that daydreaming can distort perception in a present waking state). What you believe you are seeing, feeling, and hearing may not be in a shared reality with anyone else.

Could it be that I manifested the little girl into existence? The possibility that I had created a manifestation using my imagination, will, and energy has kept me awake pondering the implications of such ability. However, I personally believe this possibility as a far-fetched, unscientific, and illogical one.

Then there is another possibility, one that really defies logic. Could it be that the spirit of a little girl, who was a former patient, decided to make contact with me in a very tender way? I do not "know" the answer to that. The answer to that question falls away from knowing, and enters the realm of belief. Nevertheless, I can say in all honesty, that it was a profound experience, and one that I will never forget.

I would like to mention that this personal experience took on more meaning later on. When reviewing the audio data from that investigation, we found a couple of recordings of a little girl's voice; in one she was singing.

14 SENSITIVES AND CLEANSINGS

Sensitives (Mediums and Clairvoyants)
The degree of psychic capabilities for each of the above are all over the internet, and not all of the articles agree exactly. Without adding my interpretations, I will simply say that these extraordinary people have an ability to receive and/or deliver communications with unseen entities. Though I have emphasized throughout these pages the importance of documentation, using people with these talents on investigations, if they are available to you, are incredible assets.

Be advised: there are people that claim talents greater than they possess, and misunderstand or misrepresent themselves. Potentially, the cause of those voices in their heads might not be of psychic origin. If you employ such a person on your investigation, they are part of your team essentially. Know the person and their capabilities well before you invite them to join you and your team for the night.

When you use a psychically gifted person on an investigation, isolate him or her from the bulk of your team; pair that person with one investigator for the duration. The reason that you do this is that if the psychic is in communication with, or can sense, particular entities, they will be releasing specific information that could compromise investigative objectivity and/or independent investigative integrity. In other words, if the psychic is communicating with what he or she believes is an old man named Jim, and all of the investigators are tagging along listening intently, then they will have developed preconceived notions that will limit their objectivity. It is much better to let the psychic do his or her thing with just one investigator to document as much as possible, and allow the other team members to investigate with conventional means. Once you review the investigation data, compare notes to see if there is evidence that backs up the psychic's impressions or communications. If you find that you have received video or audio data that supports the impressions that the psychic received, you have some interesting and compelling evidence.

Cleansings

Though this practice has little to do with the activity of paranormal investigating, I will address some considerations and concerns here. Many paranormal investigative teams investigate and perform house cleansings clearings, and/or blessings. I admire the process that people follow to identify problems, formulate a solution, and see the solution through to completion. However, I have several reservations about the cleansing practice.

A complete solution to a particular problem requires understanding of the complexity of the problem; it requires clear definition of variables within the problem. Though well intentioned, a paranormal investigation team, even one with a gifted psychic, is not going to determine the clearly defined problem. The investigative team's personal beliefs and a limited understanding of the physical and spiritual nature of the known universe often limit the conclusions that define the scope of the problem. Yet, even without a full understanding of what the problem is, a cleansing ritual commences.

Cleansings can take many forms depending on the spiritual or religious beliefs of the person conducting the ritual, or beliefs of the property owner who desires a solution to what they consider a problem. More often than not, the practice involves burning sage, cedar, or incense, salt for purification, and praying or chanting of some sort in an effort to banish, or in some cases help a spirit "cross over." I want to make myself clear here: I mean no disrespect to the practice or beliefs of those conducting such cleansings, but this type of psychodrama seems to be a one-size-fits-all solution to paranormal problems. If these cleansings do work, meaning solve the problem, to what degree do they work? Do these cleansings remove the one entity that was wreaking havoc on the homeowner? Alternatively, do they remove all of the spirits, good or bad, within the location? Is a cleansing of a location the spiritual equivalent of a tactical surgical strike, or is it the equivalent of burning down the house to get rid of the ants?

When it comes to the effectiveness of a cleansing, it seems that the results are determined by the degree of paranormal activity after the ritual. In cases where the amount of activity has decreased after such a ritual, it is generally assumed that the cleansing was successful. The demon, harmful spirit, or negative energy has left the property and is causing no more trouble for the occupants. Are there other possible conclusions to a successful cleansing? I would say yes; there are many, and they are not limited to:

1. The paranormal activity might not have been a constant situation. An occurrence here and there, random events, are difficult, if not impossible, to measure accurately. The decided halt in paranormal activity might be slack water in the ebb and flow of the cycle of activity.

2. It is very possible that there was not any paranormal activity to begin with. The observed activity was merely perceived as paranormal. In such a case where the occupants of the establishment "believe" that they are haunted, and, "believe" that the only course of action to extinguish the activity is a cleansing, then, most likely, the cleansing would be "believed" to be successful. Since there was no real activity, the faith in the ritual to remove the non-existent activity would validate the lack of subsequent activity.

3. If the nature of the paranormal activity revolved around knocking sounds, electrical surges, strange smells, etc., and those occurrences decreased or dissipated after a clearing, it is possible that the conditions that caused the perceived activity changed. The electrical problem might not have been within the structure, the problem that was causing irregular fluctuations might have been caused by faulty equipment elsewhere. A sewage blockage that caused noxious smells might have cleared. The rat that was living in the wall causing scratching and knocking sounds finally died. However, if these items righted themselves after a cleansing without the occupant's knowledge, it might be assumed that the cleansing had everything to do with the apparent lack of activity.

4. Another possibility I would like to propose is that the activity was valid paranormal activity; however, one of the occupants of the location might be causing it. The human mind is an amazing thing, and its capabilities are not fully understood. If a person with exceptional psychokinetic abilities strongly believes that ghosts exist, it is quite possible that the person will be subconsciously manifesting the behaviors that a ghost might create. If that belief is strong enough to create such activity, and the belief that a cleansing ritual is the only possible solution to remove the activity, then a cleansing ritual would most likely be successful.

So far, I have only mentioned a few possibilities for a successful cleansing, but what about a cleansing that is unsuccessful? A cleansing ritual was conducted, but the activity remained the same or increased. Would this mean that the ritual was held improperly? Not necessarily.

When performing a cleansing, it is already assumed that an entity that has been causing problems needs to go. This might not be the solution to the real problem. A cleansing is not going to fix an electrical problem, a structural problem, a plumbing problem, ground toxicity problem, or a hoax. That is why it is so important to identify clearly the nature of the paranormal problem.

Many people warn against holding a cleansing of a location if you are not fully capable. The warnings suggest that you might open yourself up to harm, or make matters worse. I have no inclination to believe or disbelieve these types of warnings. I suspect that these warnings originate from similar mindsets that warn against using Ouija boards and the like. I merely present these warnings to you so that you know they exist, not as my personal endorsement.

One last thing I would like to mention regarding cleansings, whether they are successful or not, and it involves rights. If these entities truly exist and are self-aware, then should they have rights? Are we, as humans, so egotistical to think that our existence has priority over all other corporeal and non-corporeal beings that we become aware of? So, if an entity is causing sufficient problems for living occupants in a dwelling, why are people so determined that it is the entity that needs to leave? Should not the possibilities of coexistence and understanding be explored first, assuming that the entity was proven a non-corporeal, self-aware, and rational being? Every living thing has a right to exist regardless of our understanding. Whether you refer to these entities as ghosts, spirits, angels, demons, inter-dimensional beings, or just "entities," the same rights should apply. And though I do not have sufficient evidence that would prove that such entities exist, I do not engage in cleansings, clearings, and similar rituals for that reason, and urge you to consider all of the factors mentioned here before you do.

15 MOTIVATIONS

In chapter two, I challenged you to look into your own motivations for becoming a paranormal investigator. In chapter four, I briefly touched on motivation on behalf of a homeowner or business owner on initial contact, and recommended doing some background checking. I would like to address the subject of motivation a bit more in-depth, because motivations will influence everything in your investigative experience, and in your life.

Everything happens for a reason. This statement is found in countless spiritual and religious contexts, and it is true from a scientific standpoint, as well. You might remember a child saying (or you may have said this yourself at some point in your childhood) that someone did something to you "for no reason." Whether you have heard this statement or made it yourself is unimportant. What is important is that it was not true; there is always a reason. The reason for a particular desire or behavior has everything to do with motivation.

When you looked into your own motivations for becoming a paranormal investigator, you might have answered simply. Your reason(s) might be that you are simply curious; you imagine that you would enjoy the thrill of a paranormal encounter, or that you have always had the feeling that there was something more in life to experience that was not tangible. If you are honest with yourself, no matter what your reasons are to get into this field, they are valid. Understanding the motivations of someone contacting you for a paranormal investigation is no different, and sometimes they are significantly more complex.

Being able to comprehend the true motivations of a home or business owner that reaches out for your services is vital to truly grasp the whole of the situation or problem. This understanding will affect everything that you prepare for and how you conduct your investigation. It will also affect the development of your investigative goal. The motivation(s) for someone to contact you for an investigation is/are almost limitless. Though this is hardly an all-encompassing list, the motivations might include:

1. A legitimate claim of paranormal activity; this is the best-case scenario. A credible person has personally observed events that he or she cannot explain within a reasonable understanding of physical laws of a common, so-called "reality." The motivation of this person to contact you is to get help in documenting the activity and receive some possible explanations of how and why the activity is taking place. In this particular instance, the investigative goals are clear. Planning for and conducting the investigation can be focused on particular events.

2. Mistaking extraordinary occurrences as paranormal; this common scenario must be handled with tact. Like the person with a legitimate claim, this motivation is the same; they would like to get documentation and/or explanations. Though there is not much difference in the motivation of the homeowner that contacted you, there might be more subtle cues based on the claims that would indicate that this situation might not be paranormal at all. With experience dealing with people, you might be able to notice certain behavioral idiosyncrasies or world-views of the client that might provide insight on how they perceive certain events. For instance, if the client is reporting that an entity that has been attacking him by hitting him in the stomach, you might ask if he has seen a medical professional to see if there is a natural cause for such pains. From that person's viewpoint, a strong belief that a harmful spirit is attacking him is just as logical as having an ailment, and the earnest request for help is just as convincing. You may plan and conduct an investigation, but at some point you are probably going to figure out that the problem is not paranormal. How you discuss the lack of findings with your client when you suspect that physical or mental issues are the crux of the problem requires the utmost delicacy. If you are not a medical doctor or mental health practitioner, you cannot make a legal diagnosis, but you can recommend that they see an appropriate professional. Be prepared for strong reactions when making such a recommendation, especially if the client is convinced that the cause is paranormal.

3. They just want to talk and they view you as the expert. Unbelievably (pardon my sarcasm), people have opinions regarding the paranormal. By virtue of having your team's name out there as a paranormal investigator or team, people will view you as an expert. Inevitably, someone who wants to discuss his or her experiences with you, or has significant insight into a particular facet of the paranormal, will contact you. Some people will contact you because you deal in paranormal events, and chances are, you will listen to them non-judgmentally. Others might contact you out of loneliness, curiosity, or because a ghost told them to do so. How you handle this unsolicited form

of contact is completely up to you. However, I recommend that you remain professional, kind, and understanding.

4. Purposefully misleading contact; it happens. To think that everyone that contacts you to discuss their paranormal situation or to request an investigation is honest and respects what you do would be naïve. In chapter four I briefly discussed those contacts that have hidden, usually legally/financially motivated, agendas. However, there are purposefully falsified contacts made for other reasons. The driving force behind a purposefully misleading contact is not always mean-spirited, but always self-centered. For the most part, these people do not know, or possibly do not care, how much time and effort you put in to answer calls for help, interview clients, prepare for and conduct investigations and post- review of all that data. They are simply interested in satisfying their own various needs.

There are people, and chances are you probably know a few, that cannot have enough drama in their lives. They may have seen a television show or movie where paranormal activity is going on and the occupants are so helpless to solve the problem that they seek out a paranormal investigative team. The motivation of these people is to fulfill a need to be the center of attention. These sorts of people have concluded that occupants of the "haunted" establishments get much attention and pity from the investigators and from their friends, so they invent such a situation in order to play that role. For the most part, the people described here may not be aware of how much of your time they are wasting. To them, you are just playing a role in the imaginary play they have manufactured to fulfill their needs. It is a bit sad, but some of these people are so engrossed in the psychodrama they created that they start believing it.

Other people seem to get a kick out of watching you spin your wheels and waste your time for their own amusement. What may have just started as a simple joke, contacting you with an elaborately detailed account of paranormal claims, might end up with you spending hours upon hours trying to help the deceitful client. If you do not catch on to the fact that the client has made you the butt of a joke, any investigation that you conduct is "for entertainment purposes only." This would be the paranormal investigative equivalent of a prank call carried too far.

Hoaxing would be the next step for such a client by setting up a series of devices designed to simulate paranormal activity. If you have been so convincingly misled and start an investigation and then come across such a device, you have a couple of choices:

1. Halt the investigation. Pack up your equipment and chalk it all up as a learning experience. You might alert other investigative teams in your area of your experience with the client as a courtesy. These types of elaborate pranksters are rarely satisfied with pulling the wool over one team's eyes.

2. Use their devices for training. If they have constructed an instrument that emits EMF, test it with all of your detectors, and find out if they are all reading the same values. Though the device might not be reliable enough to calibrate your equipment, it might provide an understanding on which ones are more sensitive. If you have a member on your team that is in training, allow him or her to investigate the area without informing them of the hoaxing devices that you are aware of. Was the member able to detect the device's effects on instrumentation? What conclusions were they coming up with? After the trainee has conducted a sweep of the area, you can point out the apparatuses and their intended effects. Hoaxers of this degree are rare, but if they have gone through this much effort to try to fool you, use their efforts to your and your team's advantage.

So far, I have addressed you and your client's possible motivations. Within the paranormal puzzle there is the possibility of another party whose motivations deserve consideration. What are the motivations of entities? Let us assume for a moment that entities truly exist and are conscious of themselves and living people around them. What could be their motivations to establish contact with you? Essentially you are a stranger to them. Though you may have conducted research into the claims of activity and you are able to call out the entity by name, assuming that name is correct, you are still a stranger. How do you react when approached by a stranger, especially a stranger asking questions? How would you react to a stranger coming into your home, walking around asking personal questions?

With the established assumption that entities indeed exist and are aware of themselves and their surroundings, I would like to propose a few positive motivations for them to interact with you.

The need for companionship or social interaction might represent the best-case scenario. The entity reaches out to you by actions or words in an effort to communicate and establish a rapport with you. In such a case, you might receive intelligent, direct responses, and walk away having that positive feeling of connection.

On a similar positive note, there is the entity that peacefully contacts you wanting or needing something; though this could be misunderstood and possibly unnerving depending on the form of contact. This is a positive motivation for connection. The entity needs help and it believes you are capable of providing that help. I often wonder if many frightening experiences are simply misinterpretations of intent based on the type of contact; suddenly feeling a cold grip on the shoulder of an investigator might be perceived as a scary event. Perhaps the entity is unable to speak, and touch is the only option it has for making contact with the living. Therefore, even if the initial contact is well-intentioned and positively motivated, the receiver perceives the contact as hostile or malicious.

Keeping the same assumption above, there would also be negative motivations depending on the individual entity and its particular circumstances. To assume that every entity that wishes to make itself known to you is well intentioned would be as foolish as assuming that every strange dog running toward you is only motivated to lick your face. Motivations, positive or negative, stem from a need or desire. The affect, from the recipient point of view, from a negatively motivated entity varies with the condition of need or want.

Suppose for a moment that entities actually gain strength from particular emotions. Obviously, if pleasant emotions were the "food" of particular entities, then contact with the living would be positive. Conversely, if negative emotions gave particular entities strength, then people interacting with the entities would have negative experiences. For instance, an entity that fed on the emotions of fear or sorrow would, most likely, create situations that would cause fearful or sorrowful situations within its sphere of influence.

Hatred is also a motivating negative force. If an entity hates one or two occupants, or people in general, they would be free to act out its malevolent behaviors with little concern for consequences.

Whether you are dealing with a "good" entity or "evil" entity is purely a matter of perspective; if the interactions are pleasant or the living benefit to any degree, the entity is generally considered, "good." However, if the perceived interactions are negative, whether the intent of the interaction had malice or not, the entity is generally labeled as "evil." In the previous example where the entity fed off fear, the entity would be practicing a survival; sort of a predator-prey situation. Much like a hawk diving in on a rabbit, from the rabbit's point of view, the hawk is evil.

Understanding the motivations within the paranormal cast of characters is vital to understanding the paranormal picture. It is never just a matter of recording that bump in the night. The puzzle is solved by collecting the data surrounding all of the events, including the event that brought you to the location, and discovering the motivation behind each one.

16 END NOTES

Though you may have the best intentions of helping your clients solve their paranormal problems, you must keep in mind that you have a life, too. Chances are that you are not a professional full-time paranormal investigator, and you probably have a paying job that will support you in this field of study, or hobby, whatever you decide to call this activity. Just know that it can devour most of your spare time if you allow it to.

Even though you will be looking for places to investigate and want to remain as flexible as possible, you still need to guarantee that you have your own life matters to attend to. This means that you need to maintain some personal distance from your paranormal investigation activity. Your interactions with clients and the public should remain at a professional level. All contact with clients, the public, and other paranormal teams, should be filtered through a team email or specific phone number that is only used for your investigative activities. With regard to interaction with your clients and the public, I offer two pieces of advice:

1. Never give your personal contact information to a client. Once you do, you have just informed them that you are available 24 hours a day, 7 days a week, even if you never speak these words. Regardless of your initial impressions of the client, they might later surprise you; receiving phone calls at 3 AM demanding that you come over and solve their paranormal situation has happened. Keep your communications through official channels and avoid such problems.

Maintain distance from the problem. Getting too personal with the client makes you lose objectivity. Create no emotional attachments to the client or the paranormal problem that they are dealing with. Think of it as a job, and do your job to the best of your ability.

I have roughly sketched a picture of paranormal investigating for the beginner within these pages. I have kept the depth of the implications of investigating very shallow so that you can explore more deeply on your own. The more research that you conduct on the subject is going to make you a better investigator and the data that you gather remains realistic and meaningful. You are going to make mistakes, as everyone in this field has, so take each one as a learning experience and improve your methods and techniques. Above all else, be safe!

Good luck and happy hunting!

ABOUT THE AUTHOR

Michael White is a retired military service member with experience in surveillance, preparing mission briefings, and media reconstruction of mission events. As a paranormal investigator, he has adapted these skills and procedures to the pursuit of researching and documenting paranormal phenomena. Michael resides in Silverdale, Washington and is a writer of ghost stories.

Made in the USA
Charleston, SC
05 September 2013